Jocasta's Children

Jocasta's Children
The imprint of the mother

Christiane Olivier

Translated by George Craig

R

Routledge
London and New York

First published 1989
by Routledge
11 New Fetter Lane, London EC4P 4EE
29 West 35th Street, New York, NY 10001

Photoset by Mayhew Typesetting, Bristol, England
Printed in Great Britain by Richard Clay Ltd, Bungay, Suffolk

British Library Cataloguing in Publication Data
Olivier, Christiane,
Jocasta's children.
1. Children. Interpersonal relationships
with mothers. Psychological aspects –
Feminist viewpoints
I. Title
155.4'18

ISBN 0–415–01434–4
0–415–01435–2 Pbk

Library of Congress Cataloging in Publication Data
Olivier, Christiane.
[Enfants de Jocaste. English]
Jocasta's children / by Christiane Olivier; translated by
George Craig.
p.   cm.
Translation of: Les enfants de Jocaste.
1. Women–Psychology. 2. Women and psychoanalysis.
3. Freud, Sigmund, 1857–1939. I. Title.
HQ1208.04313 1989
150.19'5–dc19   88–18298

Contents

Contents

Translator's preface

A psychotherapist who had been given a copy of *Les Enfants de Jocaste* asked me, not trusting her own French, to read it and give an opinion. There was neither urgency nor importance in the request, so that, a few days later, when I was waiting in a pub for a friend, it seemed perfectly natural to have a quick look through the book, and perhaps settle the matter then and there.

The friend was late, and perhaps that was just as well. Casual inspection turned into deep involvement. Just how deep became clear when I found myself staring, eyes filled with tears, at the page, and needing to make a huge effort to reroute a sob towards the safety of a cough. It was a close-run thing, for these weren't the tears of the maudlin or sentimental adult but of the bereft child. I had suddenly been faced with a fragment of the ancient past, a reminder of the terrifying deserts of experience that dot our early years. Whatever else this book was or did, I saw it could reawaken the immediate sense of those; and that was no small strength.

That first judgement has survived many rereadings. The book sets off other and very different responses too, but, whatever the local emphases or preoccupations, whatever the shifts in focus or form, it retains that capacity to cut straight through, at unpredictable intervals, to the fears and fantasies of the child: the child that we are, not the child that we remember or are knowledgeable about.

But the book is unusual in more than one way. Anyone who has even the slightest acquaintance with the works of French psychoanalysts will be aware of their difficult, often rebarbative idiom, and the way it conveys to the reader what can seem like a contemptuous challenge. Here that is to be found only as an example of how *not* to write or speak about the vital issues that psychoanalysis addresses. Christiane Olivier's own writing is open, excited, erratic, immediate. Indeed, so marked is the contrast with orthodox psychoanalytic texts that hers can begin to look superficial, lightweight: pop psychology rather than adequate commentary. It is invariably when that sort of thought has begun to form that she releases one of those insights or observations that pin the reader to her or his chair. It is invariably when we find ourselves saying 'Of course, that's really only true for women/men/the French/some other Other' that she directs the beam at us.

The movement of the argument is spiral. The key notions are continually re-presented as part of a steadily widening discussion that moves from analysis of cradle-experience to reflections on socio-political ideology and practice. But always the main focus is on the effects of a particular (and, she contends, disastrous) kind of mothering: the one that we in Europe have evolved.

The intensely personal, first-hand nature of the arguing puts it closer to eager, even impatient speech than to systematic exposition. But then that mode itself, for her, is bound up with the ideology whose falsity she wants to show. The translator must try, then, to follow her in her changes of tempo and tone, her preference for questions over statements, her yokings of private and public, her inventions and her repetitions.

It seems overwhelmingly worthwhile.

Introduction

Psychoanalysis has its language: sophisticated, complicated, designed to drive away any of you who are not analysts, to throw you off the track, blind you with science.

Feminism has its language: high in colour and imagery, sexualized, made to allow you in, to let you understand, even if you're not a feminist, most of all if you're not a feminist.

Then there are those who don't feel at home in either because in any event they refuse to be extremists.

Must stay somewhere between these two languages; not cut myself off from you by taking up the first, not swamp you by talking the second. Must talk instead the language of the centre, which leaves out neither emotion nor intellect. Must be woman *and* analyst, that is, keep up the two extremes, keep together the orderedness of words and the disorder of feeling, refuse to be either more woman or more analyst, refuse to split or specialize.

For too long I let 'them' set me up with 'their' words which I didn't recognize and couldn't understand. Why did I go on letting them talk about me when I wasn't saying anything about them? Well, I've decided to talk about 'them' too, to take a turn at defining them, from within a theory written by a woman in and through a woman's words, a woman's fantasies.

They can keep their 'Name of the Father': that's their business. I'll have the 'Shadow of the Mother'; I'll focus on the language of transference so as to find out how big a place the maternal has in it. If at the outset psychoanalysis was written in the masculine, is it not time now to read it in the feminine? If Freud could see woman as lacking in 'maleness', feminists are finding that man is strangely unendowed with 'femaleness'.

In a time when men and women want to shorten the list of their differences, they must first take stock of the distance that separates them, learn where and when it starts; they must go right back to what was the earliest language of all. For, long before the transferential, there was the transmaternal. And the transmaternal, it seems, is what is radically different between the sexes.

In other words, everyone on the analytic couch talks about mother. But how? What do they say unconsciously? It is these questions that will be taken up here, by way of the story that I as a psychoanalyst find myself being told. It is a story which doesn't always square with what Freud told us. He was a man and I am a woman; the 1880s were his time, mine is the 1980s . . . .

Voices off

Sigmund Freud: 'You predict that, after I've gone, even my mistakes may well be worshipped as holy relics . . . Far from it. I believe that my successors will be quick to knock down anything that is not securely buttressed in what I leave behind me.'[1]

François Roustang: 'Thus there is no analytic theory in advance on which one can lean, but rather a possibility of theorization in deferred action, which, although necessary, is never guaranteed.'[2]

Robert Stoller: 'Something has gone wrong in Freudian theory.'[3]

Luce Irigaray: 'Psychoanalytic discourse on female sexuality is the discourse of truth. A discourse that tells the truth about the logic of truth: namely that the feminine occurs only within models and laws devised by male subjects.'[4]

Robert Pujol: 'The woman's secret desire is to hide the fact that the man's body represents the unbearable rivalry of difference.'[5]

Hélène Cixous: 'They have committed an antinarcissism in her! A narcissism that only loves itself if it makes itself loved for what is lacking!'[6]

Robert Pujol: 'Woman represents the generalized castration which speech inflicts on the living creature, and, insofar as she lacks a penis, she represents the absolute alienation of language.'[7]

Hélène Cixous: 'Where is she, where is woman in all the spaces he surveys, in all the scenes he stages within the literary enclosure?'[8]

Jacques Lacan: ' "The" woman can only be written with "the" crossed through.'[9]

Hélène Cixous: 'Man's dream: I love her – absent, hence desirable, a dependent nonentity, hence adorable. Because she isn't there where she is. As long as she isn't where she is.'[10]

Jacques Lacan: 'There is a *jouissance* proper to her, to this "her" which does not exist and which signifies nothing.'[11]

Hélène Cixous: 'Moreover, the "dark continent" trick has been pulled on her: she has been made to see (= not see) woman on the basis of what man wants to see of her, which is to say, almost nothing.'[12]

Luce Irigaray: 'How can I say it? That we are women from the start . . . And that their history, their stories, constitute the locus of our displacement.'[13]

Anaïs Nin: 'I want a different world, a world not born of the need for power which marks the man, and which is at the root of war and injustice. We must create a new woman.'[14]

Hélène Cixous: 'There will be some elsewhere where the other will no longer be condemned to death.'[15]

The conspiracy of silence

Queen: Have you forgot me?
Hamlet: No, by the rood, not so:
          You are the queen, your husband's brother's wife;
          And, – would it were not so! – you are my
          mother.

Hamlet, III. iv. 13–16

Laius/Jocasta . . . Jocasta/Oedipus . . . Oedipus/Antigone and Ismene – there we have the Greek tragedy that spans the origins and end of the unhappy hero whom Freud chose as the model for every human destiny. Out of this tragedy, with its variety of major and minor characters, Freud took only Oedipus, the son who loved his mother and slew his father. He describes at great length Oedipus' feelings, wishes, remorse. There is no end to what he has to say about Oedipus; but who is there to take notice of his accomplice Jocasta? Jocasta and her desire, which drives her to sleep with her own son, flesh of her flesh, with the man who has the sexual parts that she, a woman, does not.

Can she really be forgotten, this Jocasta, embodiment of the ancient androgynous dream all humans have known? She who closes over the unfillable gap in Being, she who does away with lack, who abolishes castration: can she be left in the shadows?

Yet that is where she was left by Sophocles (and Freud after him). Not entirely, though. Her appearance in the play may be a brief one, but the effect of the small number of words she does utter is to stupefy Oedipus and spectators alike:

'God keep you from the knowledge of who you are.'[1]

Perhaps after all Jocasta did know something about Oedipus' origins, about the death of his father and about the crime which she was still committing with her son. A Jocasta who was guiltier than Oedipus? An Oedipus who was the plaything of Jocasta and her desire?

But has the race of Jocastas died out? Freud has nothing to say. Why this silence round Jocasta? This silence which has actually prompted belief in the innocence of mothers. Are mothers able to escape a destiny which their children cannot?

Those stories we psychoanalysts are told, in which the mother never seems absent, or innocent either. Putting and keeping a distance between children and their fathers – argued for by men and acted on by women, who alone hold power in child-rearing.

Laius out of the way and Jocasta taking up all the space round Oedipus: the classic tableau – a tableau that is as much part of the modern drama as of the ancient tragedy.

Did Jocasta live incestuously with her son of her own knowledge, of her own will? Are today's women aware of what they are doing when they take first place with their children? Do they know what they are giving rise to in their sons and daughters?

These women who say quite casually of their sons: 'He's going through the Oedipal stage'; it never seems to occur to them to think to themselves, even for a moment: 'I'm going through my Jocasta stage.' If Oedipus is thought of as the universal model of man, maybe it's time Jocasta was thought of as the eternal myth of the woman-and-mother.

As a woman and a psychoanalyst, I could hardly fail to be drawn to this character missing from Freudian theory, or to notice that this theory, on which my analytic practice is based, lacks any female referent.

How could I avoid seeing that if the men I constantly run into are Jocasta's sons, the women are her daughters? What lies behind all this? What does it imply for me as a woman? In this area the whole of Freudian theory needs to be reinvented. I have reached the point where I can no longer stand apart from my woman patients, or play dumb in the time-honoured fashion. In this book I will not separate what I *am* from what I *know*; and I can say out loud and clear that the things I hear from other women on the couch put me in touch with a feminine order that I recognize as my own.

As a result, I shall be talking alternately about these women and about myself, in an effort to situate us differently from the guidelines laid down for us up till now by psychoanalysis. It has become necessary to rethink the theory of the unconscious, with the help of women and the benefit of their words. The days are past when men could simply invent women to fit their own specifications, or rather the specifications of their need to dominate.

Sure enough, psychoanalysis is notably revealing of what men *expect* women to be. What is far less sure is that it gives any kind of account of what women actually are. As Luce Irigaray rightly says: 'Up to this point, the main concepts of psychoanalysis, its theory, will have taken no account of women's desire.'[2]

If women could be reduced to being no more than man's fantasy, the converse is and was theoretically possible: it might have been men who were reduced to being no more than women's fantasy! We may join Germaine Greer in regretting that psychoanalysis had a father but no mother![3]

If there is indeed no place in this sexist society for the women who talk to me, then I can find no trace of my desire in a theory based entirely on male premisses.

Freud was the first to adopt a scientific approach that was ego-centred, unlike any other: instead of focusing on something out there, in the external world, he took himself as research topic and set the findings against the great myths of humanity: those of Oedipus, Moses, and Michelangelo. Clinical case studies lie alongside literary and artistic analyses; we sense that Freud is seeking a single law common to man as he was and as he is. Thus the case of 'Little Hans' goes with 'A childhood memory of Leonardo da Vinci', and the case of Daniel Paul Schreber with *Moses and Monotheism*.[4]

But for the most part, with the exception of Dora, they are male figures. Perhaps that's only natural. Freud was, after all, a man. Had he not every possible encouragement to direct his enquiry at himself? How could he have enquired into the woman that he never was?

And so, when it came to defining *her*, he never went beyond observing how a woman in 1880 lived; a petty-bourgeois woman from a conventional family where roles were immemorially settled. It is very obvious that at that time such women had 'a certain place' in society, rather than 'a place that was certain'. Now we women find ourselves confronted by a psychoanalysis which, quoting chapter and verse (supplied by Freud, who took them from his family and acquaintance), allows us only a strangely reduced place. Here is Freud writing to his beloved Martha on 15 November 1883:

> But I believe that all reforming activity, legislation and education, will founder on the fact that long before the age at which a profession can be established in our society, Nature will have appointed woman by her beauty, charm and goodness, to do something else.[5]

Surely he is talking here like the worst kind of anti-feminist, making it clear that he is set on running together women's sexual attractions and their place in society – creating in the process an unholy mess from which women are only just beginning to emerge.

The mere fact that he got to a point where social and sexual could be merged indicates that he must have done some strange repressing, and gone along some unlikely roads, all leading to the famous 'dark continent' of feminine sexuality.

It was not Freud who brought in the inferiority of women, even if many feminists try to persuade us that it was. But it has to be said that he did everything possible to explain it, make it logical and therefore inevitable. The real trouble is that, once Freud comes on to the scene, the inferiority which could be observed socially took on a scientific appearance; his feminine equations were taken for universally familiar adages. Women still bear the scars of them.

Benoîte Groult is correct in claiming that: 'Women were perhaps just about to take off on their own when a catastrophe befell them: Freud.'[6]

What can a woman analyst say about the Freudian attempt to adapt women to men? What else than that God made Eve from Adam's rib, and Freud made feminine sexuality from male libido. Is it not one and the same myth? Are we not dealing with male fantasies in a patriarchal society in which, throughout history, men have been considered superior, and women kept down?

It is not without significance that Freud always chose myths from Greek or Latin – and therefore patriarchal – civilizations. If only he had glanced at civilizations different from these! He might have come across 'the other feminine myth', with its witches and Amazons, its founding goddesses, its warlike Walkyries. Our image would certainly have been influenced by that; above all, our role would have been thought about differently.

When Freud turned to the great myths of antiquity, he always, as if by chance, lit on civilizations where the man held the front of the stage. By narrowing the distance between the man in the street and the hero, Freud certainly conferred on the former a touch of eternity. But, oh dear: the unconscious he gave him was that of a nineteenth-century, middle-class man who, like the rest of the men of his time, couldn't imagine any place for women outside the social inferiority where he saw them confined.

He saw women fall silent in the presence of men and, on the strength of that, concluded that they were incapable of intellectual sublimation. He watched them seeing to the needs of men and got the idea that they were masochistic. He saw them looking after children and immediately confined them to motherhood, where they would be able to make good what they lacked (in line with the famous equation: penis = child).

And women now are noticing, after a long period of silence, that if Freud left behind a statue of man that stands on the securest of bases and looks out towards sublimation, his statue of woman is a monument to mindless maternity–fecundity. But this is wholly inappropriate to today's women, who are mothers for a while (and no longer as a matter of course), and women always – and who are not given to confusing, even for a moment, these two aspects.

Women cannot be reduced to the mothers that they agree to be, for a few years, within the family; any more than men can be identified with the fathers that they are for their children. The immediate result of that is that women are now bringing the sexual function back to its proper place, which is not connected with reproduction (that is what 'they' tried to put over on us), but with sexual pleasure. Over the past few years, women – and it has meant overcoming no small range of prejudices, Freudian among them – have won the right to orgasm without reference to motherhood.

And women have the feeling that they are coming out of a very strange prison that was invented by men; man-the-psychoanalyst being merely one among them, though perhaps the most insidiously dangerous. For he has notably strengthened the bars of our cage, by passing off the birdcatcher's lust for capture as the bird's pleasure in being captured. (The immemorial dominance of men has, by way of the supposed masochism of women, become the woman's inborn wish.)

The system has finally been shown up for what it is, the truth finally revealed; and the reduction that Freud subjected women to, by basing himself on the family and society of his time, is now being applied to him by women who make bold to say that he, with his patriarchal Oedipal ideas, was bound to reduce them to silence.

Most commonly, when feminists today want to attack the phallocratic system, they focus their anger on one man: the father of psychoanalysis. Just as Freud used his own Oedipal experience in order to get at that of humanity as a whole, women now start out from 'his' Oedipal feelings and 'his' misogyny in order to explain the misogyny of mankind.

This inductive step, patented by Freud himself, is still bringing results: at the present time Papa Freud seems to be guilty of just about every crime that has been committed against women over the centuries.

In order to square his account with his mother, Freud had to attack all women, and now they are all for digging him out of his grave and getting their own back: an eye for an eye, a tooth for a tooth . . .

Open any feminist work and that, it seems, is what you'll find. Freud figures as Public Enemy no. 1, ahead of anyone else: writers, sociologists, doctors. Psychoanalysis, we are told, is a dangerous, infectious disease, but fatal only to women. Would it not be more appropriate to say rather that up till now it has been one-sided: dealing only with the masculine, even though this masculine can only be established as an independent entity if it is counterpointed by something called woman or femininity? The only image of us is the one that the man needs in order to preserve his supremacy as man. What are these male imaginings to us? Might we not be better employed in doing some defining on our own account – as for example of what we look for in men? We have paid a terrible price for allowing ourselves to be defined by the other. It is time we did the talking, about ourselves.

If the function and the objective of the masculine are those of penning in, pinning down, closing off the feminine, then we want nothing to do with what men say. We must define ourselves. The duty of women psychoanalysts is just that: to write 'the other psychoanalysis'.

And the way we shall do so is by going back to Freud and making a fresh start, repudiating his anti-feminism. For I think that outright rejection of Freud's discoveries, which is what feminists want, may well mean denying ourselves access to an approach whose main lines have already been laid down. The first stages of that approach can be of use to us, even if we cannot accept where it eventually takes us. Our best chance of finding out where Freud made his basic mistake about the sexuality of women is to go back over the ground he covered in accounting for the development of girls.

For it is very much the case that, when it came to women, this pioneer of latent truths, this tireless investigator got it hopelessly wrong. The more his account is correct in everything to do with men, leaving no room for doubts or denial, the more his thoughts on women must be reviewed through different eyes, like stolen goods that are finally to be restored to their rightful owners.

That is where I as a woman want to take up my position: at the very centre of this shambles of male fantasies and expressions about femininity, most of which, by virtue of their esoteric nature, have the effect of keeping women out of male preserves. Are people aware even that such frequently used items of analytic vocabulary as superego, sublimation, orgasm, and phallism more or less leave women out altogether?

If Freud had been less taken up with the idea of bringing feminine sexuality down to the inferiority observable in society at large; if he had listened to his women patients more and invented them less, he would never have set foot on the famous 'dark continent', that terror of both sexes. If he had even talked of an 'uncharted shore', women would doubtless have felt the urge to set their feet on this inviolate beach and leave their mark on it.

Ever since Freud left us, male sublimation has proceeded apace; today, the extreme complexity of psychoanalytic writings is aimed only at diverting attention, which, endlessly pursuing words, loses sight of meaning.

Involvement in the war of psychoanalytic phonemes has too often masked the underlying sex war. And because it has been neglected, ignored, this sex war is now raging. I am not saying that this is the fault of analysts, but they are partly responsible. You can't spend part of every day going along with the unconscious of each of the sexes without reaching some conclusions on how they work and what they want.

Granted we have nothing decisive to say about cure (that is, in the end, the patient's choice), there are perhaps certain conclusions that we can draw concerning the male and the female unconscious in general.

Following the example of Freud himself, who established the

connection between pathology and normality by writing *The Psychopathology of Everyday Life*, perhaps our job is to write *the psychopathology of the everyday couple*, as we see it inside and outside our consulting rooms. Surely it was just such a project that Freud was referring to when he wrote:

> For we do not consider it at all desirable for psychoanalysis to be swallowed up by medicine and to find its last resting-place in a text-book of psychiatry . . . As a 'depth-psychology', a theory of the mental unconscious, it can become indispensable to all the sciences which are concerned with the evolution of human civilization.[7]

And indeed, psychoanalysis has gone on to have a prominent place among the human sciences and in education. It crops up all over the place, whether tucked away in a popular magazine like *Elle*, or openly displayed, as in some recently published autobiographical writing. The analytic way has become, if not the 'royal road to the unconscious', at least a humble path that many of us find ourselves taking.

One might well wonder (and a great many women have done so before me) at the fact that, amid all this analytic outpouring, there has been no attempt to work out proper bearings for the male–female unconscious within the perspective suggested by Freud himself towards the end of his life. For Freud was concerned that psychoanalysis should get beyond pathology to a study of human behaviour in general.

There is for example the relationship, decried by women, of dominator and dominated, in family and society alike. Would it not be possible to study it where it first took shape in the woman's life – and even then not with men but with the 'other' woman: the mother? Must we not turn our attention once again to the mother–daughter relationship, if we really want to understand something of what goes on later in relation to men? For what goes on then is merely repetition. But repetition of what, precisely?

This is where Freud broke off, at the very edge of this virgin 'continent' whose soil, he believed, must surely be ploughed by his successors: 'But at the end of her development, her father – a man – should have become her new love-object . . . New problems . . . now require investigating.'[8]

If, in a first stage, Freud was content with a discourse which, though in appearance logical, belittled us as women, surely in a later stage he reduced to rubble all that he had laboriously built up. Did he not recognize his own inability to give an account of the development of the little girl? Surely he was foreseeing what part women would play in this research when he wrote to Marie Bonaparte, a woman analyst of his own time: 'What do women desire?'

So I am going to come out of the silence that is for the most part the lot of women and psychoanalysts. In actual fact, I'm well aware that the only kind of argument that I as a woman would be licensed to put forward would be a treatise on child-rearing, considered to belong as of right to women. I refuse to go along with this mother-and-child business, for I am not sure (you will see later why) that the upbringing of children should be left to women, in spite of the express wishes of some of them, and against what men believe.

The Oedipal experience has done such strange things to us all that, before we get down to talking about our roles, we would do well to take a look at our various histories . . . and our histories take us right through the Oedipal experience. That experience, then, is what we shall be talking about: bringing out its logic, identifying its terrible traps and dead ends. The Oedipus complex that Freud went through and told us about was that of a little boy living in a society where the man's function was 'social', and the woman's, 'familial'. If the functions are switched round, or simply shared, as feminists are suggesting, what bearing will it have for the child of each sex?

In short, how far can an analyst be a feminist? If feminists now are uncovering the sexist effects of the Oedipal experience at the social level, it is the responsibility of women analysts to uncover its origins and development through the individual unconscious. If women are uncomfortable, uneasy, it is the duty of any woman analyst to look for the cause of that in the history of the feminine unconscious as it is revealed in analysis. Language has been stolen from women; it is time now to give it back to them, to listen to them and not cover our ears, as most men do when they find the even tenor of their ways disturbed by this voice from elsewhere.

As Hélène Cixous writes:

It is time to change. To invent the other history. There is 'destiny' no more than there is 'nature' or 'essence' as such. Rather, there are living structures that are caught and sometimes rigidly set within historicocultural limits so mixed up with the scene of

9

History that for a long time it has been impossible (and it is still very difficult) to think or even imagine an 'elsewhere'.[9]

Faced with the female psychoanalytic silence on the subject of feminine sexuality, and granted the endless masculine babbling about it, one is driven to wondering whether there just aren't any women to 'dare' (as Freud dared) to remember their childhood, and why women seem to have opted instead for the memory that men have of them. For sometimes their boyhood memories reappear, transposed into resentful complaining, in our lives as women.

How long shall we go on allowing the male Oedipus complex to rule our lives as women? How long shall we go on putting up with a situation where men pay us back what they owe to Mother?

2

In the beginning was Freud

> In the face of such uncertainty it is most unfortunate that Freud insisted on proceeding so far in constructing a psychology of women.
>
> Kate Millett, *Sexual Politics* (London, 1971), 178

Why is Freud so virulently attacked by women? Why Freud rather than some other man? We are well aware that he is not the only sexist, the only phallocrat, the only enemy of femininity. We are indeed; but he alone built up 'his' truth into an objective-seeming science, 'his' sexuality into a universal sexuality.

In psychoanalysis we find a conception of woman that has been dreamed up by a man; a woman such as many men might wish her to be, but one perhaps unrelated to what 'woman' really is.

From Freud onwards there occurs a distortion of feminine sexuality which women now are challenging as totally unrelated to them.

What has to be remembered is that, if there hasn't yet been a woman to remember the story of her early girlhood, there was, at the outset of psychoanalysis, one solitary man who recalled his early boyhood with his mother . . . Let us not forget that Freud had been adored by his mother, who was young, pretty, desirable, married to a much older man, and with a son who gave her satisfactions which must have greatly puzzled young Sigmund himself. From this life with his mother, this little boy, when he became a man, drew conclusions concerning masculine development which have never yet been successfully challenged. It would appear that the analysis he gave was pertinent indeed. But when it comes to women, it is a different story.

The clear pattern of development in the boy seems to have drawn him into a sizeable trap, for in the earliest phase of his work he strove to establish the girl's development as *symmetrical* with the boy's. This led him into some strange flights of argument concerning little girls, since he wanted to establish symmetry round a fundamental asymmetry (that of the sexes), and since for him male supremacy seemed unquestionable (which may raise a smile nowadays). He had no end of difficulty in working out a theory – given detailed exposition as early as 1905 in the *Three Essays on Sexuality* – which seems to us now to be packed with improbable notions, of which the two most obvious are: penis envy, and the renunciation of the clitoris.

Penis envy, or envy for the parts one hasn't got

One of the earliest claims we come across in the *Three Essays* on the subject of infantile sexuality seems wholly unexceptionable: 'It is self-evident to a male child that a genital like his own is to be attributed to everyone he knows.'[1] But it opens straightaway on to a question: what do little girls believe? These girls who also know no genital apparatus other than their own, are they capable of imagining a different one? Now Freud, determined to confer primacy on the male sex, answers the question, with no discernible logic: 'The assumption that all human beings have the same (male) form of genital is the first of the many remarkable and momentous sexual theories of children.'[2]

And in case we hadn't understood he adds, later on: 'We might lay it down that the sexuality of little girls is of a wholly masculine character.'[3]

Or again: 'It would even be possible to maintain that libido is invariably and necessarily of a masculine nature, whether it occurs in men or in women.'[4]

Here, in this primacy of the male, is a rather striking convergence between the earliest analytic theory and the dominant ideology. And, more curiously still, it is a theory to which Freud will remain attached all his life. Penis envy, set off by the girl's suffering from not having a male sexual organ, is a datum which regularly recurs throughout Freud's writings on infantile sexuality in girls. Whether it is in the *Three Essays* or the later papers, the form of words is practically always the same:

Little girls do not resort to denial of this kind when they see that boys' genitals are formed differently from their own. They are ready to recognize them immediately and are overcome by envy for the penis.[5]

They notice the penis of a brother or playmate, strikingly visible and of large proportions, at once recognize it as the superior counterpart of their own small and inconspicuous organ, and from that time forward fall a victim to envy for the penis.[6]

And from this envy, Freud will go on to draw conclusions that are congruent with his views on women in general. What a shame that his premises should be so dubious:

The psychical consequences of envy for the penis, in so far as it does not become absorbed in the reaction-formation of the masculinity complex, are various and far-reaching. After a woman has become aware of the wound to her narcissism, she develops, like a scar, a sense of inferiority . . . Even after penis-envy has abandoned its true object, it continues to exist: by an easy displacement it persists in the character-trait of jealousy.[7]

Freud must have been confident indeed of possessing the only worthwhile sex (or needed desperately to persuade himself that he did) for him to set up envy and jealousy of the boy's genital as the mainsprings of psychological development in girls. For, as a little reflection shows, it is by no means certain that every little girl is in a position even to see the 'large penis' of brother or cousin. For if the penis is large, it must be the case that the boy is at least adolescent; and would he, at that age, agree to display it?

Add to this unlikeliest of scenarios that a girl would have to be oddly blind, or have a strange imagination, to see anything in the boy's sex that remotely resembled hers. It's hard to see how the girl's 'slit' and the boy's external 'appendage' could ever be equated.

The whole thing is a figment of the imagination of a man absolutely set on establishing a comparative relation between the sexes, instead of establishing that the evidence pointed to a radical difference between them.

We have to wait until a different research reaches us; by a woman this time, and with a very different message. In 1974 Luce Irigaray finally decided to abjure this Freudian dogma that bore so little resemblance to reality, even if it meant that her Freudian colleagues would not understand.

No doubt she was breaking up the pattern of received ideas, transmitted all the way along psychoanalytic doctrine; no doubt she was rather too brutally upsetting the calm certainty established by Freud as to the supremacy of the male gender.

Luce Irigaray challenges the claim that femininity is founded exclusively on envy and jealousy of the male sexual organ. She works patiently through the whole history of this famous 'primary', evaluative gaze directed at one sex by the other. She takes a dim view of the fact that this recognition of difference leads on to a devaloriz- ing of the feminine.

> Why does the term 'envy' occur to Freud? Why does Freud choose it? Envy, jealousy, greed are all correlated to lack, default, absence. All these terms describe female sexuality as merely the *other side* or even the *wrong side* of a male sexualism . . . 'Penis envy' . . . means nothing less than that the little girl, the woman, must despise *her own* pleasure in order to procure a . . . remedy for man's castration anxiety.[8]

In short, women, according to Luce Irigaray, are seen as losing or having lost something so that men can be spared seeing themselves as losing, as unprovided with. For it is very much the case that man is not 'all', any more than woman is; with nothing to show but vestigial breasts and missing womb. And this woman analyst goes on to say, with a logic that is now unmistakably feminine:

> The *desire to have it* would confirm man in the assurance that he has it . . . If it were not so, why not *also* analyse the 'envy' for the vagina? or the uterus? or the vulva? Etc. The 'desire' felt by each pole of sexual difference 'to have something like it too'? the resentment at being faulty, lacking, with respect to a heterogene, to an other? the 'disadvantage' mother nature puts you to by providing only *one* sex organ?[9]

And so envy, it is argued, is not after all specifically feminine but common to both sexes, and bears on the sexual attributes of the 'other'. This is amply confirmed by children's play, where each child will try to see what the other one has. And it looks as if each one, as a result, feels distinctly aggrieved at discovering that he or she is missing something that the other one has. Hence those games of pretend, where the placing of cushion or ball varies with the sex of the child.

All through his disquisitions on penis envy, we find, don't we, Freud mentioning 'his own' envy of the breast, femininity, maternity – all those things that men have dreamed of having since time began, and which, since literature began, the poets have sung? There is no end to the celebration in literature of our curved neck and bosom, our breasts, our tiny waist: in short ail the things which men don't have and envy us for having. The locus of male envy is indeed the bosom, continually hymned, extolled, bedecked with all the qualities of loving-kindness, fullness, and softness attributed to mothers.

But does the man's 'breast envy' allow us to infer the existence of 'penis envy' in the woman? What is all this new psychoanalytic stuff that suddenly comes along and sets itself up against so many hundreds of years of poetry, of literature in general? And can anyone show me that other poetry, by women, which sings the charms of men? When are we to see the new feminine poetry or literature that takes as its subject the male body and the penis, in all their alternating strength and fragility?

For there are no two ways about it: the male organ, which Freud taught us was the object of such envy by women, hardly ever appears in the graphic arts or in literature unless the artist is a man – Greek statuary, Etruscan pottery; the paintings of Picasso, Chagall, Dali; the novels of D. H. Lawrence, Henry Miller, and so on.

But on the distaff side: a blank; silence; the word unheard. This precious, eminently coveted object has failed to attract the pen or the brush of any woman (with the very recent exception of Benoîte Groult, and her description of it is anything but flattering).

No, it is the men who have something to envy. They are the envious ones, the jealous ones, but, by an astonishing reversal of the facts, we find ourselves saddled with their shortcomings and inadequacies. As Annie Leclerc so rightly points out: 'We had a sex that was so rich in events, adventures, experience that men might have paled with envy at the mere mention of it – and what happens? They have actually managed to turn us, with all our wealth, into the envious ones.'[10]

The same writer goes on unhesitatingly to relocate envy, inviting us to share in the endlessly renewed joys of the female body. And it may well be that this penis envy that has been attributed to women is merely the obverse, the reverse of men's breast envy.

Breast, which we all of us came to know at the very beginning, in our mother's arms. Breast, which, later, we all lost, and have always dreamed of finding again. Loss that only women are capable of making good, both because it is there on their own bodies and because they see that men have something that can be given to them, in the same way that long ago their mother 'gave' it. For what men see as virile aggression, women receive as generous breast (penis = breast). 'When we make love, I am full of you, enchanted by you, by the song of you wandering near, the murmur of you wandering far; but not taken, not ravished: *there*, more than ever there, and full, more than ever full.'[11]

This is how women express themselves when finally they take the liberty of talking about their sexuality without reference to what men may make of it. Not ravished or possessed or raped, but enchanted, filled, marvellously fed: that is how women feel during love-making. Of course they need the man's penis, but they don't envy it or wish to keep it. Not at all: what they want is for the other to give it to them. What they want is to make it welcome, to take it in, sometimes to keep the fruit of it.

No, in this area, the 'underequipped' one is the man, for he has no means of making good the primary loss, except by looking at and touching as many breasts as he can (cf. men's magazines and the photos in them). Men are, quite simply, avid for breasts, and this unquenchable longing of theirs they have managed to plant on us, deceiving both themselves and us at the same time.

In the end, behind the apparent contrast between the gentleness in the writing of men poets and the aggressiveness of feminist writers lies one and the same fantasy, one and the same envy: envy of the maternal breast, forever lost, forever sought by men as by women. But to take this as an axiom is to challenge the entire phallocratic theory of sex. Annie Leclerc again:

> They invented sexuality in its entirety in the absence of any sound from our side. If we invent our own, they'll have to rethink the whole of theirs. Men don't like women; not yet. They go after them, they desire them, they subdue them, but they don't like them. But women hate women.[12]

Now this opens up a whole new field for psychoanalysis: it is necessary not only to rethink feminine sexuality, but to explain the hatred women have for 'other women'; to explain, not jealousy and envy of the penis but aggressive desires directed at the mother, first of the women that the little girl meets along her way.

Giving up the clitoris

The second major element of Freudian theory bearing on feminine sexuality will, since it concerns the uses of the clitoris, be still more radically exposed in all its inadequacy; not only because it was poorly argued in the first place and lacked any genuine anatomical basis or clinical backing, but because all the physiological and scientific experiments carried out since then have produced evidence which contradicts the theory.

Advances in scientific research and the availability of statistics (non-existent in Freud's day), taken altogether, make short work of a ramshackle system whose main purpose was simply to subordinate women once more to men's desire. Under that system, genuine female orgasm was further subordinated to internal male penetration, to the detriment of external clitoral sensations, which it labelled secondary, incidental, or neurotic – an argument which men keep using so that they may act on the basis of their own desire and in a way that shuts out any possible demand from women for their pleasure.

In the age of data processing, no-one can defend for very long any thesis that has no connection whatever with the real. But that is what Freud tries to do.

With theory as his instrument, he attempted to perform a veritable 'mental clitoridectomy'. What is at issue is nothing less than getting women to give up part of their anatomy because men consider it masculine. There was to be no entry to feminine sexuality except by way of renunciation, a prefiguring of all those other renunciations to which we will be bidden by Freud later on.

> If we are to understand how a little girl turns into a woman, we must follow the further vicissitudes of this excitability of the clitoris. Puberty, which brings about so great an accession of libido in boys, is marked in girls by a fresh wave of repression, in which it is precisely *clitoral* sexuality that is affected. What is thus over-taken by repression is a piece of masculine sexuality.[13]

Where might we not be led, if we are not careful? As well say that the female entity has no independent existence among humans in the natural state; that it is only an imitation based on masculine anatomy; that it can come to have existence only if and when it disclaims certain parts of its body which have been found too 'masculine'.

None of this will be lost on our brave and lucid advocate, Luce Irigaray, who writes:

> So we must admit that THE LITTLE GIRL IS THEREFORE A LITTLE MAN . . .
>
> In the beginning . . . the little girl was (only) a little boy. In other words THERE NEVER IS (OR WILL BE) A LITTLE GIRL.[14]

To boost his chances of being believed, Freud thinks up a change of erotogenic zone, with an accompanying transfer of clitoral sensation to the vagina, which *has* been labelled feminine, doubtless because it is useful for the man's pleasure. No doubt about it, 'the woman does not exist', which is what Lacan says, pushing things further still. 'Freudian', he calls himself. I should just say 'Oedipal', that is, carrier of death-wishes towards women.

Here is Freud once again explaining and rationalizing the necessity of giving up the clitoris and vesting pleasure in the vagina, the receptacle for the man:

> Before this transference can be effected, a certain interval of time must often elapse, during which the young woman is anaesthetic . . . When erotogenic susceptibility to stimulation has been successfully transferred by a woman from the clitoral to the vaginal orifice, it implies that she has adopted a new leading zone for the purposes of her later sexual activity. A man, on the other hand, retains his leading zone unchanged from childhood. The fact that women change their leading erotogenic zone in this way, together with the wave of repression at puberty, which, as it were, puts aside their childish masculinity, are the chief determinants of the greater proneness of women to neurosis, and especially to hysteria.[15]

Ill-conceived equating of the clitoris with something masculine, which sets Freud off on the wrong track; for from that point on, women are reduced to experiencing orgasm in only one part of their sex: the part sanctioned by men. So how can 'she' know climax other than by identifying herself with the desire of the 'other'? The very definition of hysteria; the only orgasm available to women is hysterical.

Hysteria is all she has left. Is it hysterical psychosis? Or neurosis?

As a result of suspension, within a suspension, of the economy of her primal instincts. She will do 'as' she is asked . . . And hysterical miming will be the little girl's or the woman's effort to save her sexuality from total repression and destruction.[16]

It does indeed appear that women, starting out from their renunciation of this desiring part of themselves, move into the area of mime, of alienation feigning the sexual pleasure of the other. And not the least puzzled by all this will be the men themselves: is she really having an orgasm, or is she pretending to, the way she has been shown?

If even the detail of her sex has been 'pre-scribed', there has been no 'scribe' to record in comparable detail the woman's orgasm, and that is just what baffles the man, for he is not entirely sure that he has done a good job of inventing women; and as long as she won't tell him, he cannot know.

An orgasm reduced to that of the 'other', located in the same place as that of the other; or double orgasm eluding the man's grasp? Has the man contrived to make the woman a prisoner of his penis, the highest term in the phallocratic system; or does she slip away down the shadowy corridors of a secret orgasm? And is this double orgasm the effect of a double organ or of a double fantasy (for him, a hysterical fantasy; for her, an auto-erotic fantasy)?

Questions men keep bringing up, with themselves and with us. Between the miming of the desire of the other and the actuality of her own desire lies the whole space of the 'feminine secret' which nags so at the minds of men: 'Ever since we've been begging them – last time I mentioned women analysts – begging them on our knees to try to tell us about it, well, not a word! We have never managed to get anything out of them.'[17]

Fury of the man who cannot know in the other's stead, as he suddenly notices that, although he has taken everything away from her, 'she' alone has control of what she knows. And yet had he not taken every precaution to keep her out of all this business of orgasm, and of understanding of orgasm? 'There is a *jouissance* proper to her, to this "her" which does not exist and which signifies nothing. There is a *jouissance* proper to her and of which she herself may know nothing.'[18]

But maybe it's dear old Freud's infinite patience, as he comes back once again to this everlasting clitoris (everlasting for her, puzzling for him), and saying the opposite of his usual theories: 'When at last the sexual act is permitted and the clitoris itself becomes excited' (What? So the woman hasn't altogether given it up, in spite of all your wise counsel?), 'it still retains a function: the task, namely, of transmitting the excitation to the adjacent female sexual parts, just as – to use a simile – pine shavings can be kindled in order to set a log of harder wood on fire.'[19]

Now that really does bring you up short. Can this really be Freud speaking? Might there be a contradiction between the scientific research worker, his mind set on having done at any cost with feminine sexuality, and the man, who can see a part for the clitoris to play in coitus (perhaps Martha's was still active, even if she was the wife of Sigmund Freud?). After first being miles from the truth, do we not see Freud miraculously close to researchers today? The very expression used by Masters and Johnson is virtually the same: they talk of the clitoris as 'setting off orgasm' – and they are sexologists!

The clitoris observed scientifically – during actual coitus, not just as imagined in a phallocratic society – turns out to be an organ with a high proportion of Pacini cells (sensitive cells which can be found in several parts of the body, but preferentially in the clitoris and surrounding areas: the labia minora and labia majora).

It has been shown that there is no orgasm without the clitoris being involved to some degree. The vagina, by contrast, has been defined as devoid of sensitivity in all but its bottom third. So women had been making great efforts to reach climax with an organ unsuited for the purpose – unless they had actually all along been using their clitoral sensations and keeping quiet about it. There will be no knowing until women have lost their shame at talking about this organ which fails to win universal approval.

And, as usual, shame has melted away fastest in America. That is a country which has not been crushed by hundreds of years of patriarchy, and we are sometimes made sharply aware of the fact. Only recently we have had from them the Hite Report,[20] which, because it leaves it to women to do the talking about their own sexuality, does finally demonstrate the importance the clitoris has for them, since they see it as the indispensable first element that initiates all further sexual pleasure.

The confusion sown by psychoanalysts has vanished away at the hands of, first, biologists, and later, women. Woman, whose sex had been 'stolen away' from her by psychoanalysis, is at last getting it back.

But what do you think of the cunning old rogue who once said: 'If you want to know more about femininity, inquire from your own experiences of life, or turn to the poets, or wait until science can give you deeper and more coherent information.'[21] Well, the old rogue was none other than Freud himself, discouraged by the complexity of the feminine problem, and showing a touch of the prophet, for we have just had decisive scientific information. As for the poets, their answer has been available for generations. All that remains is for us to inspect our own analytic experience.

And indeed the story of Freud has amply demonstrated that we cannot count on men to relate our experience. There has been only too much damage done to women's state by letting others speak in our stead, by trying to slip unnoticeably into a speaking voice that is different from ours.

We must as women be genuinely Freudian, and act on his final piece of advice. I say 'final' because, between the *Three Essays* of 1905 and the *New Introductory Lectures* of 1933, Freud had thought long and hard about this supposed symmetry between the sexes, and several times gone back on what he had said earlier, opening up for us at many points new directions of research which, oddly enough, women have been so far reluctant to take.

Oddly enough or logically enough? For we are very well aware why women have kept quiet for so long, and why, even now, when they do start to speak out, they are conscious that they will incur something like rejection by men.

Women are only just starting to show themselves as they are, and not the way men want them to be. Perhaps men will no longer accept them? Perhaps they will be driven back on their own resources (in solitude or in homosexuality)? There are risks about taking a gamble, which we have been taught to measure rather than to overcome. And very often women are still afraid of the death-bearing wishes directed at them, and prefer silence to death.

3

Dark continent or blank page?

> The 'Dark Continent' is neither dark nor unexplorable. It is
> still unexplored only because we have been made to believe
> that it was too dark to be explored. Because they want to
> make us believe that what interests us is the white continent,
> with its monuments to Lack.
>
> Hélène Cixous, *The Newly Born Woman* (La Jeune née),
> trans. Betsy Wing (Manchester, 1986), 68

After what reads to us today like a long speech for the prosecution
against woman, do we believe that it actually was her trial that Freud
was trying to bring about? Had he not rather, unwittingly, spoken
only about man, never really about woman? Had this woman who
was the obverse of man any connection with the women whom Freud
had been seeing and hearing for years in his daily round? Did he
know anything even about these women? He seems to have cast some
doubt on that himself, writing one day to Marie Bonaparte: 'The great
question which has never been cleared up, and to which I have been
unable to find any answer, in spite of thirty years of investigation of
the feminine psyche, is: What do women desire?'

And so, in spite of all that he had said and reiterated, he felt no
further forward, at the end of his life, in understanding the problem
of woman. He was quite willing to admit as much publicly in 1925:
'We know less about the sexual life of little girls than boys. But we
need not feel too ashamed of this distinction; after all, the sexual life
of adult women is a dark continent for psychology.'[1]

There: the dreaded word is out, the word that has become so

familiar; a subjective notion that becomes a subversive one, for this continent is dark for Freud (as we have seen, the poets deck it in the most sumptuous colours) only because it frightens him, just as anything that was unknown could frighten him. We have only to remember his phobia about travelling abroad (the episode of the journey to Rome that didn't come off). How much worse it would be when the journey took him to that 'strange, exotic creature' which man sees woman as.

This darkness puts us in mind of night, with all its more or less terrifying fantasies, evil spirits, heart-stopping visions, ghastly nightmares. In the night anything might happen to us: defenceless, we are given over to the invisible powers which, by day, we can so easily rout. Freud reveals in this his original terror of woman, which had up till then been so carefully masked by a theory whose main objective was to keep 'her' down. Which amounts to saying that the concepts he formed concerning women were based, not on feminine facts but on masculine fears.

Nor is he alone in expressing reductive views of women. Remember the notorious 'Woman is not all' of Lacan,[2] which indicates that he too has known the fear that she might indeed be 'all'; this woman whose belly is heavy with promise of more, whereas man knows that there will only ever be one of him.

From this frightening dark, Freud moved to the blank, blind mystery unexplored and unexplorable, secret not uncovered. Does he not, in connection with women, evoke Minoan–Mycenean civilization? Does he not persistently go back in time, as if gripped by panic at what he might find if he focused on the woman who was constantly there beside him? As soon as women are in question, it's either pure invention or panic. Freud swings between dark and blank, black and white, unformulated and incapable of formulation:

> Everything in the sphere of this first attachment to the mother seemed to me so difficult to grasp in analysis – so grey with age and shadowy and almost impossible to revivify – that it was as if it had succumbed to an especially inexorable repression.[3]

But why this insistence on women? Might men have a clearer memory of the womb, the arms that bore them? Clinical practice suggests nothing of the kind.

No. Quite simply, if the Freud of the *New Introductory Lectures* has got beyond the usual shutting out of woman, he still feels obliged to keep her at a distance: cellar (where it's dark) or attic (blank and unreadable under the white dust of the years) will always be better locations for her than 'face-to-face'. How could he have contemplated any face-to-face with the woman whom he had first adored, then put aside in favour of another?

Specifically masculine dilemmas which for years drove Freud to argue for a theory which put an ever greater distance between men and women.

Is it mere chance that it was only after his mother had gone (Amalie, Freud's mother, lived to a great age, and only died in 1930; he himself was by then 74 and would die only a few years later) that Freud, in 1931, during a new lecture on feminine sexuality, dared at last to change his attitude to women and put forward new questions about them? Finally abandoning his lifelong struggle against the mother and the wife, no longer relying on the age-old arguments like social inferiority, social and maternal role, he actually gets to a point where he stops using their feminine sexual conformation to explain their subordinate status within a patriarchate. Now come the real problems, which Freud had not yet addressed. For if women are no longer thought of as rejecting what they have and envying what men have, what is it that women do have? What is their life actually like? Belatedly, Freud gets to the primordial question: What sort of life does the little girl have when she is alone with her mother?

At last he is looking at this creature that he had always preferred to think up rather than see as she was: of the axioms laid down for the boy, none fit her. In particular, Oedipal status, on which the entire masculine structure rests, has no existence for her. The principal dictum: 'a child's first object choice is an incestuous one' does not apply to the girl brought up by a mother of the same sex as herself.

> We have an impression here that what we have said about the Oedipus complex applies with complete strictness to the male child only, and that we are right in rejecting the term 'Electra complex' which seeks to emphasize the analogy between the attitude of the two sexes.[4]

So here is Freud, in the twilight of his days, recognizing that he has done no more than lift one corner, one side of the curtain on the Oedipal tragedy; Jocasta and her daughters have been left in the shadows, where the spotlights don't reach. But by now Freud has neither the time nor the courage to put up the lights again, any more than to reread Sophocles, who himself had touched on the great difference in situation of girls and boys, as well as the plight of girl-objects who had become unmarriageable because of their father's crime:

> Creon, you need not care
> About my sons; they're men.
> But my two girls – so sad and pitiful . . .
> Creon, have a thought for them![5]

Sophocles may have marked off a difference, but Freud had shown himself unable to explain it correctly, and in the end he concludes: 'It must be admitted, however, that in general our insight into these developmental processes in girls is unsatisfactory, incomplete and vague.'[6] How can we not be surprised: can this be the same man who was so eager to establish the initial symmetry between boys and girls? Here he is now admitting that there is no such thing as symmetry between the sexes, and then saying that he has no idea about development in girls. On the basis of these two observations, he has more questions to ask:

A further question arises: what does the little girl require from her mother? What is the nature of her sexual aims during the time of exclusive attachment to her mother?[7]

The phase of exclusive attachment to the mother, which may be called the pre-Oedipus phase, possesses a far greater importance in women than it can have in men.[8]

In little girls the Oedipus complex raises *one problem more* than in boys. In both cases the mother is the original object; and there is no cause for surprise that boys retain that object in the Oedipus complex. But how does it happen that girls abandon it and instead take their father as object?[9]

With the small girl it is different. Her first object, too, was her mother: How does she find her way to her father? How, when and why did she detach herself from her mother?[10]

What a lot of questions! What a lot of lines of enquiry opened up for those who would come after you! 'Finally, I am no longer alone. An eager crowd of fellow-workers is ready to make use of what is unfinished or doubtful.'[11]

And if there is one thing that went on being doubtful for Freud, it is how the girl develops into a woman. If there is one thing to which he continually came back to revise his ideas, it is feminine sexuality. But to have believed that his successors were going to take up what was left unfinished, and especially to grant women a less unfair sexual status, was naïvely Utopian in a society so deeply marked by male power. And in fact what followed was much worse than the beginning had been. Far from there being any rethinking on the subject of girls, things went from bad to worse. *Penisneid* (penis envy), grew in importance until there was nothing left of women but this overwhelming envy:

> The essence of the female dream is the 'little other' – in this case, the brother – and the essence of this little other is the phallus.[12]

> Women become mothers in order to make good this Penisneid, and the desire of mothers is to go on being mothers . . . For women, all other substitutes pale in comparison with the equation penis=child.[13]

Quite so. We are back with this equation, which has nothing new about it, since it had already been put forward by Freud: penis=child. It looks as if this is what gentlemen find most acceptable, even if, just recently, ladies have not been entirely happy about it. Men carry on along the line of their desire: we must be kept strictly to motherhood, and kept unconditionally out of other places such as culture or sublimation. And when it comes to these, men will not mince words or hold back. Read what they have to say:

> The question of meaning, and of the meaning of life, is a masculine question. It does not arise in women.[14]

> There is woman only as excluded by the nature of things which is the nature of words . . . Only they don't know what they are saying, which is all the difference between them and me.[15]

> Woman represents the generalized castration which the word inflicts on the living creature. In so far as she lacks a penis, she represents the absolute alienation of language.[16]

Elsewhere we read (that is, if 'we' have not been forbidden to go in for reading, since it is one of the ways to sublimation): 'If women do indeed know something, is what they might or might not know of any concern to psychoanalysis?'[17]

Men as psychoanalysts have been misled by the jealousy over motherhood, blinded and deafened to all logic by *Uterusneid*. But among Freud's successors there were also women. Indeed he had appealed to them direct. Had he not written to Marie Bonaparte 'What do women desire?'? Again, speaking of the mother–daughter relationship within the transference, he had said: 'It does indeed appear in fact that women analysts – as, for instance, Jeanne Lampl-de Groot and Helene Deutsch – have been able to perceive these facts more easily and clearly.'[18]

What actually became of these women analysts? What position did they take up on the masculine view? Well, with very few exceptions, they associated themselves with the men's way of thinking. They pretended to believe in this truncated penis of theirs, this 'penis envy'. They behaved as men expected them to. There was Helene Deutsch with her 'Renunciation is typically feminine'.[19] There was Marie Bonaparte with her critical look at the clitoris, that tiny organ which was so 'temporary', and which women 'would have to' turn away from, in spite of the difficulties that would bring.[20] There was Jeanne Lampl-de Groot writing 'Feminine love is passive',[21] and later, Ruth Mack Brunswick going back to Freud's idea: 'At the start of her sexual life, the little girl is, in terms of intentions and goals, a little boy.'[22]

Why did all these women analysts, Freud's other successors, allow the error about feminine sexuality to persist, when Freud was counting on them to lay down the lines of a different theory, one which gave a more accurate account of women? There is cause for irritation, assuredly, but we could usefully remind ourselves that it was doubtless hard to be the daughter of a father as changeable with women as Freud was . . . .

For all this came very late on the scene, and only after statements so peremptory, demonstrations so amazing that women (even the analysts among them) were left speechless, plunged in stupefaction and horror at the destiny that was theirs. If you cut someone's head off, do you expect them to keep calling out their name? That is pretty well what Freud was asking his women contemporaries to do.

It is clear enough that at the end of his life Freud had it in mind to give the bird back its freedom. The feminists' reproach is that he had cut off beforehand all means of flying. And is Lacan not trying to steal language from us as well, when he says that we don't know what we're saying?

When men analysts appropriate words which they claim are theirs, it does not occur to them to think of this as theft. But in fact by doing so they are talking in our stead and stealing, not only our language, but also our sexuality, which they lock away within their male fantasies.

And if Freud woke up to the trap he himself had earlier introduced, that didn't stop it from operating just as before. For after Freud had gone, the only ideas of his that they took up were the ones which he had extensively glossed – and sometimes recognized as baseless.

Psychoanalysis has not stopped being spoken and written in the masculine, in a language that has moved further and further away from its creator. Enough to make you think that what it is directed at is something so explosive that there is every reason to hide it behind the impassable barriers of a hermetic language. Did you know that sometimes, in that language, the talk is of nothing less than cancelling the very existence of creatures sexed as women?

Were you aware that one of these men analysts, a Frenchman, has said 'La femme n'existe pas', and that he loves writing 'la femme' just for the pleasure of stroking out the 'la', which assigns us to the feminine gender, on the pretext that this gender has no right to speech?

Dear Sigmund Freud

I am writing to let you know that, ever since you left us, most of your heirs and successors have failed to take up your last suggestion, and that your final reflections have been consigned to the attic of psychoanalysis, where I happen to be today, with all your papers scattered round me. Just now I am rereading your last lecture on feminine sexuality, dating from 1931, and I am absolutely delighted by the freshness of approach in it, compared with the endlessly rehashed psychoanalytic pap we are usually fed.

I notice that along the road we were to take you left some of those little white stones which might have led us back to father's house, instead of being eaten up by the sexist ogre-man, who has never seen fit to heed your last warning, and has, because it suits him, preferred to use against us the early part of your research, which deals with our supposed sexual inferiority.

Do you realize that this man, when he is angry, commonly talks of sending us 'back to our mother', but never 'back to our father', for in fact we have never actually lived with our father, even though we shared the same house. First among our homes, still, is that of our mother: is that not what you explained to us was constitutive of our deeper personality, and could cause awkwardnesses with our future partners? 'The husband . . . was meant to be the inheritor of her relation to her father, but in reality he became the inheritor of her relation to her mother.'[23]

You had even found a name for this first home: the 'pre-Oedipal stage'; but all that brought us was still louder reproaches from your successors at our not belonging to the masculine Oedipal house; and that has kept us out of a great many things. Is it not reasonable to think that, if you were to return today, you would put as much energy into protecting our pre-Oedipal stage as they do into blaming us for our lack of Oedipal experience?

Perhaps you aren't aware that, at this very moment, the idea is taking shape in women that men might be affected by *Uterusneid*, and that that might be the origin of their jealousy, their all-out war against the female sex, and their campaign on behalf of the child. It has to be said that *Penisneid* has been called in question by the fact that, very often nowadays, women decline to have children, preferring instead other activities. Are these activities also instances of *Penisneid*? There is a whole host of new problems to look into, and all one can say is that the 'discontents' of civilization seem all to be located round the issue of the place to be given to the child, since the birth rate is falling, a fact which is causing our governments no small anxiety.'

That, or something like it, is what a woman might write to Professor Freud today. That is, if she hasn't been taken in by the feminist hatred of that gentleman. For it's not so much on him that the blame should fall as on his successors. They betrayed him, the women joining the men to sing in chorus the hymn about the penis that was too small and the inferiority of women.

And then in analytic milieux, the 'in' game is still, is it not, this famous *Penisneid* – a game that men find far more amusing than women do. 'They' pretend to laugh along with the men, for fear of being left out if they don't play by the rules (the men's rules). But it is beginning to look as if masochism in women isn't what it used to be. Women are asking for different games, with different rules; games where the man's penis isn't necessarily the prize. After all, did

Freud not discover the rules underlying many of the games we had up till then played in all innocence? Among the best-known games do we not find the one with the cotton reel (in which the child invents a symbolic representation of its mother's absence by an object which it throws away, then immediately brings back)? And then the game of Freudian slips (where our mouths let us down by saying what we actually think, and not what we are expected to say), not to mention the dream game (night-time is full of dark corners, substitutions, deaths that could make our lives easier)?

If we read Freud's last writings with more care, might we not find the beginnings of the rules governing the game that the woman must play? Do we not find, among the essays on sexuality, a hint of some sort of game between mother and daughter: the pre-Oedipal, feminine game of hide-and-seek? What paths, what rules does the little girl follow in order to get out of her maternal hiding-place? What could she see from inside it? Will she, after that, ever get into the 'trespassers-will-be-prosecuted' grounds of the masculine Oedipus complex? Will it be with her father? Her brother? Her friend? What are the results of her long stay in the 'dark' hiding place? 'Dark', as Freud put it, or 'blank'?

So many questions for us women analysts. For indeed, now that the lack of symmetry between the sexes has been demonstrated, is there any room for women in the Oedipal experience as defined by men? Since her incestuous object (the father) is not there with her, what does feminine libido fix on in the earliest stage? If there is no real-world object for it, will her sublimation (the redirection of libido on to other subjects) be stimulated that much more?

At last, thanks to the women analysts of our time, the files that were locked away in the attic have been brought down and reopened. We have Janine Chasseguet-Smirgel writing:

> Embalming someone is not the same thing as keeping him alive. The only way we have of keeping Freud alive among us is to take his discoveries further, argue out whatever in them is uncertain or risky, go more deeply into certain questions, with the help of the method he bequeathed to us. Anyone who is not eaten up by hatred and fear of a dead man will have no need to waste time erecting a tomb for him just to appease his *manes* (and in the process smother him under the weight of the granite).[24]

This woman analyst puts her finger on the real problem for Freud's successors: the murder of the father – Freud's own problem, as it happens, and that of every male with his own Oedipal rival (for a fuller treatment of this subject, read François Roustang's splendid book, in which he talks of the 'savage horde' that was the experience of men analysts when Freud was alive).[25]

Men psychoanalysts, in spite of all they know about it, cannot elude the Oedipal law. But what about women analysts? What has been keeping them quiet? What fear has stopped them from going further? What if not the age-old fear of displeasing men?

The reason why analytic understanding has not evolved more, and has merely repeated itself, is that, in the field of psychoanalytic practice, all concerned have experienced the patriarchal Oedipal structure which makes men say: 'I shall not kill the father', and women: 'I shall not displease the man.'

There is nothing men don't fear from their own kind, nothing women don't fear from men: it is against the background of that difference that we must read their double silence on Freud.

For seventy years psychoanalysis has developed within a particular form: how can it speak out without outdoing the father? This form reappears in the Lacanian field, where it brutally sterilizes the neophytes of what has become a 'religion', founded by a new 'Pope', just as much beyond criticism as Freud was in his day. It looks as if the myth of the father, origin of the Law, is a pretty hardy perennial.

But perhaps there might be, stored up somewhere, rescued from the Oedipal wreck and the death wishes of men, a new, pre-Oedipal language not caught up in squaring accounts with the father – that is, not caught up with death, but pointed rather at life. Perhaps it is the emergent language of women? For if we have little enough to say on the subject of the mythical father, we have no end of discoveries to make on the subject of the real father.

What are we doing in this 'dark continent' where we have been kept imprisoned for so long? What can we see in it? Are our memories as 'blanked-out' by time as we've been told? And how much longer are we going to put up with being women without memories, having our being in a continent that cannot be described?

Somewhere between the angel's white and the witch's black, perhaps there's room for other, more feminine shades? The red of blood, of childbirth, of desire, of love?

Oedipal difference: where the trouble starts

> The Oedipus complex, however, is such an important thing that the manner in which one enters and leaves it cannot be without its effects.
>
> Sigmund Freud, *S.E.*, XIX, 257

Symmetry/asymmetry in the development of boy and girl: this is the problem that Freud has left behind him for us to argue over. His own final conclusion was: 'We have, after all, long given up any expectation of a neat parallelism between male and female sexual development.'[1]

If we take the trouble to reread his last writings on female sexuality, we shall have little difficulty, with hindsight, in seeing that there, in those writings, are the canvas, the sketch of that famous difference between the sexes which Freud always sought to trace back to a hypothetical comparing of bodies among children, whereas oddly enough he had, ready to hand, all he needed to explain it differently. If we simply put into the appropriate order what appears in Freud in no particular order, we arrive at something like the following argument:

> I will tell you, then, that the most remarkable thing about the sexual life of children seems to me that it passes through the whole of its very far-reaching development in the first five years of life.[2]

> Later, but still in the first years of infancy, the relation known as the *Oedipus complex* becomes established: boys concentrate their sexual wishes upon their mother.[3]

We see, then, that a child's first object-choice is an *incestuous* one.[4]

In the case of a boy there is no difficulty in explaining this. His first love-object was his mother. She remains so.[5]

With the small girl it is different. Her first object, too, was her mother. How does she find her way to her father? How, when and why does she detach herself from her mother?[6]

In little girls the Oedipus complex raises one problem more than in boys.[7]

It is only in the male child that we find the fearful combination of love for the one parent and simultaneous hatred for the other as a rival.[8]

The Oedipus complex, then, is the story of unconscious sexual desire: a very beautiful or a very sad story according as it is viewed as preliminary to any and every 'love-story' or as responsible for all the difficulties of love.

But, 'I will tell you', this Oedipus complex, this 'incestuous' cross-sex activity – the boy's desire for his mother and her desire for him – is a one-sided business. In our society, this incest which Freud himself pronounced 'a regular and very important factor in a child's mental life'[9] only gets into the air breathed by the boy-child brought up by his mother or another woman.

What happens to the girl during this period – the girl who, brought up by her mother and kept away from her 'incestuous object', the father, does not experience this cross-sex activity? Is it only empty air that she breathes, this girl who so often in later years will display phobias about emptiness, fearsome bulimias, shattering anorexias? There is far too much going on in that area, as far as women are concerned, for us not to pose the question: what does the girl herself want, in psychic terms, when she is given the bottle by a woman who does not desire her, since they are both of the same sex? Can the girl 'get enough' from her mother? Apparently not, since, once past this first adventure with another woman, we shall find the majority of women bound to the desire of men.

How do they get there? The history of their relation with desire must be strange indeed if it can bring them to a point where they will pay any price not to have to leave, ever again, the orbit of male desire. This clinging to the position of 'desired object' will give the woman a hard time in many ways, especially in that it will turn her into an ideal target for all the ideologies that men find convenient.

This morning a woman said to me: 'If I'm wanted, it means I'm not just nothing'. What 'nothing' can she remember, is she remembering? And who is it that is doing the wanting, if not a man? If we search about in her life as a little girl, we shall not come across any men, for there is no father hovering by the crib or the pram; and in any case it is not his job to look after her.

Is it possible not to see that, for years on end, the 'fatal' Oedipal relation simply does not exist for the girl? Where is it that she can come up against the man who desires her and her sex? Certainly not where her nappies get changed. Nor in her kindergarten or nursery school, where women hold sway.

Where are the new novels, where are the way-out cartoons (apart maybe from those of Claire Bretécher) that show us a father 'mothering' his child? Giving it its bottle, changing it when it's dirty? We haven't really got there yet, outside exceptional cases, outside deliberate opposition to local norms. For in general the man doesn't want it that way. And then, supposing he did, would the woman put up with it? The man and the woman are at one in accepting a sharing out of roles in which the man, having excluded the woman from any social responsibility, allocates to her alone the responsibility for the family. Sexism within the family, it seems, is just as intransigent as it is outside.

The woman is taken up with the child, the man is taken up with money. Who will deny that this is so, in a country where, for years now, there has been pressure for a proper salary for mothers, but where any proposal for extended paternity leave is turned down flat?

In 'Latin' countries like France, the father has not been brought up to look after the baby – his own or anybody else's. He has no part in the upbringing of the young child, and, in order to get even a small part, he has to be exceptionally obstinate, whether with his male colleagues or with his wife, who will delegate to him only part of the responsibilities that she sees as hers by vocation – by birth and by nature, as she is so often told.

Meanwhile, the man's main function, it seems, is bringing in money to feed the protagonists in the drama that is being staged under his roof without his being, for the most part, involved in it. It is always the mother who tells the story of 'the child and its neurosis', seldom the father, who leaves all that to the mother (indeed it's the only thing he does leave her). He has charge of everything else, and when he comes home in the evening what he wants is to be relieved of responsibility. It is peace that he longs for, as if he felt war unbearable, yet found it his lot to face it every day; as if all he ever came across was war, whether outside the family or inside it.

What is it about the relationship of man to war, about the war he fought long ago with his mother or the one he sees going on now between his wife and his son? Is what he remembers of the mother–child relation so awful that he won't hear of getting involved in it? Has the 'incestuous choice' he once made so marked him that he couldn't even think of standing between his wife and his son?

Is he still somehow afraid of the all-powerful mother, this man who dares not stand out against her in the control she has acquired over their son? Is it not his memories of war which now set off his longing for peace?

So it comes about that, all because of his own Oedipal struggles, he will fail to attend to his son's, and will make his daughter's impossible.

Most often he will prefer to read – to read about wars and conflicts taking place outside the family. He will bury himself in his newspaper, demand silence round the television, forcing the others to play down their personal conflicts in favour of national and inter-national disputes. What a strange sort of father this is, who has longed for children yet will not look after them! What a strange sort of mother we are seeing, who can exult in having sole charge of the children! And yet this system can't be holding up all that well, since apparently fewer and fewer parents want children.

This rigidity in family roles, this single-sex upbringing: who better to speak of them than the psychoanalyst, who keeps seeing women ending up in her consulting-room with their children, almost always on their own – and glad of it? The child's neurosis is no business of the father's, unless the analyst really insists.

This child, wanted by both parents, becomes, because it is born into a patriarchal family, the mother's exclusive 'object'. And it is a rare woman who doesn't believe that in the upbringing of the child, she is irreplaceable and the man useless!

But where did these ideas come from in the first place, if not from the man who, desperate to keep away from the woman, has divided up responsibilities into 'family' and 'outside'? Keeping the outside for himself, he has left family care to his wife, so that never again, as he sees it, will they meet on common ground.

No doubt. But surely this area that has been handed over to women is huge, gigantic, out of all proportion to the man's area? For if the man's work never moves very far from questions of status and purchasing power, is it not the woman's task to awaken the appetite – and the appetites – of the future consumer?

And did any of this cause Freud even a moment's hesitation? For whether she likes it or not, whether she knows it or not, it is the mother who sets off all the baby's sensations and intense pleasures. She it is from whom it will learn them all, even masturbation, frequently observed in children, but in fact merely carrying on from the stroking that the mother did in all innocence.

A child's intercourse with anyone responsible for his care affords him an unending source of sexual excitation and satisfaction from his erotogenic zones. This is especially so since the person in charge of him, who, after all, is as a rule his mother, herself regards him with feelings that are derived from her own sexual life . . . A mother would probably be horrified if she were made aware that all the marks of affection were rousing the children's sexual instinct and preparing for its future intensity . . . Moreover, if the mother understood more of the high importance of the part played by instincts in mental life as a whole . . . she would spare herself any self-reproaches even after her enlightenment. She is only fulfilling her task in teaching the child to love. After all, he is meant to grow up into a strong and capable person with vigorous sexual needs.[10]

Could there be any clearer way of making the point that, in anything to do with the erotic, the mother is the child's first teacher, its 'older woman'; and that the child's pleasure is a response to its mother's? In this phase, it is her genital desire which will appear as determinant of the baby's sexual awakening. Freud, it seems, after touching briefly on the question, was not interested enough in the mother's sexual life and the typical orientation of her desire towards the male sex. Faced with similar patterns of desire in children of both sexes, he hypothesized similar patterns of adult response. This put the boy and girl on the same footing in sexual terms, and Freud had to bring difference back in by way of a relatively late, and in any case hypothetical comparing of anatomies.

Whereas if one keeps one's eye on the fact that the child's mothering figure is, in the majority of cases, a woman, for whom there is no complementarity but with the male sex, it is at once clear that, for her, the son is a 'sexual object' whereas the daughter is not; which in its turn results in the boy's finding his mother a 'satisfactory sexual object', whereas only the father could be that for the girl.

This is something pointed up by Bella Grumberger, who observes, in her study of feminine sexuality:

> As Freud emphasized, the only really satisfactory relationship is that which connects the mother to her male child, and we have every reason to suppose that even the most loving of mothers will be *ambivalent* towards her daughter. A real sexual object can only be of the opposite sex, and, unless in cases where there is some sort of congenital homosexuality, the mother cannot be a *satisfactory* object for the girl in the way that she can for the boy . . . .
>
> Thus Freud says that the girl child has to struggle with the difficulty of 'changing her sexual object', moving on from the mother to the father, but we are entitled to think that the girl needs no change of object because, in the first place she has none.[11]

I am not alone in thinking that there is no moment at which the baby's sex is a matter of indifference in respect of the desire of the adult responsible for bringing the child up; or that what comes out of this confrontation between an infantile libido, intent on ensuring the baby's auto-erotic satisfaction, and a parental libido which is powerfully genital, is the establishing of the individual's male or female constitution.

The fact that the same mother, feminine in gender, looks after both boy and girl is all that is needed to bring about a fundamental asymmetry between the sexes; with one sex, the male, having an adequate object from the moment of birth, and the other, the female, having none and being forced to wait until eventually the man appears before she can find satisfaction. There can be no doubt that this unsatisfiedness has a profound effect on the woman's character.

In relation to the mother, any symmetry between the sexes is ruled out from the start, and this difference, this differentness which first appears in the cradle will become a divergence which adult men and women will find it hard indeed to accept.

By the same token, if Freud had taken his reasoning further, or simply brought together his different pronouncements – one bearing on the awakening by the mother of the child's sexuality, the other saying that the child's first 'object' is an 'incestuous' one – he would have seen that, right from the earliest moments, there is a problem facing the girl, and that if, later, she turns towards her father (a matter never fully worked out by Freud), it is because for her there is no sexual awakening possible with the mother.

In terms of the Freudian theory of the Oedipus complex as that which structures personality, the girl cannot experience this structuring, or can only experience it by a different route, without recourse to fixation on the opposite sex. There is a first stage in which no-one desires the girl's body, her sex.

Did Freud take fright at his own discoveries? For it is when we carry on his own arguments, when we follow his logic through that we come up against the stark fact that the girl has no primary love-object (rare indeed are the fathers who stay at home and look after their daughters). Let me put it this way: of all the hypothetical Oedipal women who have had their father as primary love-object, I have not, or not yet, come across a single one. What I know is daughters who have come through a relationship with their mother that had no desire in it, and then, more or less belatedly, switched to their father.

No doubt the 'new man' that the feminists are demanding, the man who will not refuse to mother his child, will father a 'new son'; but above all he will father a 'new daughter' who, right from the moment of birth, will have an adequate 'sexual object' and will no longer be driven by the devils of unsatisfiedness to the point where only perfectionism can bring her reassurance.

All this lies ahead. Meanwhile let us take a closer look at what makes up the character of the man and the woman in their relation with their mothers and within the present nuclear, patriarchal family.

The development of the boy

We start with him since it was his development that Freud called 'more logical' and easier to interpret than the girl's.

And what in fact do we see? An extremely simple infantile situation: from the moment of birth the boy finds himself exposed to the opposite sex, since his love-object is his mother, and therefore already in an elementary Oedipal position, since the famous 'incestuous' object is right there by the cradle. For the male child there will be no problem about setting up the Oedipal relation or getting into it since he is in it from the outset as a result of his birth – at the hands of a woman. Rather, it might be said, he falls into it head first, and the really hard thing for him is coming out again, getting out of this 'fatal' conjunction of the sexes while managing to keep his integrity.

For it is in her son that the mother has her only chance of seeing herself in male form. This child that has come out of her belongs to the other sex, and so the woman gets the chance of believing in that ancient dream that all humans have: bisexuality, so often represented in Greek statuary in the guise of the androgyne.

Just watch how proudly she carries this son who has come along to complete her in a way that no-one else can. Just look at the utter satisfiedness painted on the faces of all those 'virgins with child'. Surely all those Italian Madonnas are giving praise to the woman-and-mother who achieves happiness and wholeness without involving herself with the father, here banished to a myth. God the Father – a religion of men, laid down by men who recognize nothing in women but the womb that bore them. An Oedipal religion, if ever there was one, since the father is pushed out to make more room for the mother – just as he is in our own day.

Motherhood: for the man, paradise lost, haunting him so much that he wants to be master of it, be the one who decides on it. If he can't carry the child, let him at least be able to compel 'the other' to do the carrying. The woman 'gets' pregnant, in the phrase everyone knows. As if with brutal suddenness she had contracted something by accident, something unexpected that would lay her low. Men whom we have seen angrily buzzing round the problem of motherhood and abortion in a display of extraordinary violence; men who will build up the mother in order the better to put down the woman, who, it appears, has no right even to the 'desire' for a child – that is something that can be settled on her behalf. No question of her being in command. What have we not had to suffer, all because of the farrago of myths and envious feelings that the man always carries along with him on the subject of our reproductive organs!

It's a lucky woman that has a son! Is that perhaps why Lacan vengefully reminds her that 'woman is not everything'? Let her not imagine that she might occupy that position that causes so much envy in the man, who sees himself condemned to the solitary experience of single-sexedness.

No, no, don't worry: this mother is not 'everything' – even if she is strongly tempted to think that she is – for this little boy is neither her nor hers and if, briefly, she may have thought that she had the other sex in her possession, her son as he grows will not fail to take away her illusions. The longer the mother believes in her oneness with her son, the more violent and perdurable will be the opposition he puts up.

And if the first months of dependence and of mother–child symbiosis seem to hold fewer problems for boys than for girls, it is a different story as far as the next period is concerned, the period of anal opposition and self-assertion. For then the difficulties will fall on the boy who, in this phase, will have to defend himself against the maternal fantasy of completeness so as to win his independence: an independence which his mother is less than wholehearted about wanting.

The woman has unconscious difficulties about giving up the only male she has ever been able to keep by her; she whose father let her down and whose husband is more often away than at home.

There is a further difficulty (not described by Freud) which the little boy has to overcome, for he has to make his escape from the Oedipal stage *against* his mother, who does not want him to go away and leave her. This is the start of the longest but least obvious of wars against female desire; the place where the boy joins battle in the Oedipal war of the sexes. Against his own mother.

When his mother says to him: 'You'll be grown up soon enough', is she not giving expression to her desire? Is this not a way of holding on to him? Have I not known mothers who urged their sons to pull out their first facial hairs, that token of the onset of male adulthood?

Is it not on account of this desire of the mother's that the boy stays 'little' so much longer than the girl of the same age? Do we not learn from tests that there is a considerable gap in maturity between the sexes up to puberty and even beyond?

Here surely we are seeing the outward sign of the difficulty in growing up that is experienced by the boy pinioned in the maternal love-trap. Is it not the boy who wets the bed, who soils himself, who, in a word, refuses to grow up? The bad time that the male child goes through here leaves its mark on him forever, in the form of a deep fear of female domination.

It looks as if the famous 'trap' so often alluded to by men must be the trap of a symbiosis with the mother that is seen as 'imprisoning'.

Symbiosis, psychosis? At all events, a 'prison' that sets off panic in the man at the thought of any symbiosis with any other woman. Never again to be caught up in the same place, in the same desire as the woman: this is the main driving force of the man's misogyny. Holding the woman away from him, keeping her confined to areas designed for her alone (family, schooling, home) is the primary objective of the masculine campaign.

Setting up at all points a barrier, whether physical or social, between him and her, standing out against her desire in any and every way, keeping his distance by any and every means will be the man's greatest obsession. Even his sexual behaviour will be affected: he will be that much more sparing of the gestures and words that might recall something of his symbiotic lovingness with the mother.

So: no painless escape from the Oedipal stage; it will never be irreversibly achieved, and it will leave the man forever suspicious of women. Sometimes, no escape at all, which will bring mother and child to the psychotherapist's door. At this stage in the life of the human being we see three times more boys than girls (their turn will come later). That fact alone is proof of the order of difficulty that this battle with the mother faces the boy with. Where there is neurosis, it will be because the battle has made the boy into:

either a child who has been so keen to resist the mother that he has forgotten to exist for his own sake: a child dead to all desire. Such a one will be spoken of as featureless; he will speak neither at home nor at school, for the shut-down is total. In order to find out how to get rid of 'her' and her permanent desire, he has had to jettison all desire.

or a child who has turned aggressive: first with his mother, and later, by extension, with all and sundry; defying the teacher, picking fights with the boys, being mean to the girls. Wherever he is, battle is never very far away; wherever he goes, his arrival rings the alarm bell, for he is set on proving that he is the tough one. Tougher than 'her', and then tougher than anyone. What he really wants is to get the better of his mother and her control. Unstable sometimes, his increasing fidgetiness is a sign of his urge to get away from her at every moment.

And what about the father? What is he doing all this time? Where is he? Can he not see, does he not know, from having gone through it all himself, what is happening? Of course he knows. Of course he remembers. But he does not dare pull his son free of female power:

the only power his wife can enjoy undisturbed, since all other forms of power fall to him. The son has little hope of being able to count on his father to get him out of the bad time he is having with his mother, for the father deliberately keeps out of this conflict. More often than not, the first the boy will know of homosexuality will be in adolescence, with other boys of his age who are just emerging from the dangerous labyrinth. And in that context homosexuality in males acts as a defence against mothers, women, girls. Homosexuality in boys is above all a way of defending themselves against the opposite sex. We shall see later that homosexuality in girls is wholly unrelated to this way of being.

Here then, in summary form, are the general nature and effects of the problem of the male Oedipus complex; the story of the man's coming into being, as fruit of the fateful congress of the sexes, at the hands of a woman. For the man, what is born here is the tenderest of all loves, followed by the most long-drawn-out of wars. From this the man emerges showing signs of distrust, silence, misogyny; in a word, all the things women reproach men with.

It costs the man no small effort to get to the point where he can shake free of the woman he has loved best (no mother will contradict me if I say that boys are far more loving than girls) and who has loved him best. And all this is the result of cross-sex dealings within the family, where only the mother has the child-rearing role, only the mother has to live close up against her son.

In the old days there would have been grandfathers and great-grandfathers, uncles, cousins – any number of male images to break up this dangerous one-to-one. Nowadays the all-powerful mother lives with her son who satisfies all the longings she had long ago, makes up for the father who was never there and the husband who has gone away. The little boy *is* there, so he must pay for them. After all, a woman has to get a man wherever she finds him: too bad if it's in the cradle!

After the terrible struggle with this all-powerful mother, how could men possibly avoid opting for wariness in anything to do with women and their power, that power which must be held in check? How could they possibly not spend their time setting limits to our world, shutting us away with our duties and responsibilities? How could a man's love for a woman be anything but ambivalent?

Is there a man, is there a son anywhere who can say that he really has got rid of his mother? Oh, he'll have left her, all right, but how far did he get? At what age? Left her for whom? Is there a mother anywhere who could say that she has given up her son, even when she's 80? He is still 'the one', even where no word is said, even if respect for others requires that nothing be said, even if there really are brave men and mothers above reproach.

The bond that is woven in the darkness of infancy between mother and son binds them forever. When a woman marries, she can only ever marry another woman's son. Hence the clashes that go on between mothers-in-law and daughters-in-law over the same man, until such time as the younger one has a son of her own. Until she abandons the battle for the past in favour of the battle for the future with her son; this for want of the chance to hold on to the adult male, who is unavailable because invariably, mysteriously, tied up with his mother; because he is still ambivalent as between his past and his future.

Which is how the story carries on from one generation to the next: a son, secretly bound to his mother, takes a wife so that he can really get going, so that he can reproduce; but keeps his distance from her and allows her no rights beyond love-bed or child-bed. A woman without a husband, without a male equal, will foot the bill for the war in which she finds herself involved for no other reason than that she has taken over from the mother; a woman who will find in her son the only male that is really close to her. The circle has been closed, the loop looped: because the woman has been kept at a distance by her husband, she will invest in her son and prepare in him the ground of 'distance' for the other woman, the one who is yet to come. Misogyny is a crop sown by one woman and reaped by another.

The development of the girl

Now let us take a look at what is happening on the other side: while the boy is desperately struggling to break free of his mother's fondness for him, what is the girl going through – this little girl whom the same mother is conspicuously not binding to herself with hoops of steel, since in the mother–daughter relationship there is no sexual desire?

One question may be put straightaway: might the girl not be better off, since she avoids the 'fateful' combination of the sexes? Alas, not at all. But the risks are not the same, and neither are the results: if the boy finds it hard to get rid of a love-object which is 'too adequate', the terrible thing for the girl is failing to find any adequate object along her way, and so having to stay outside Oedipal relations until well into her life. The boy may start out from fusion/complementarity; the girl's early experience is of the body/mind split: she will be loved as a child but not desired as a girl's body. She is not a satisfactory object for her mother in sexual terms; only for her father could she be one.

Only the father could give his daughter an easy (because fully sexed) position, since he sees the female sex as complementary to his own and therefore indispensable to sexual pleasure (something that the mother only rarely feels about her daughter's sex, for, outside exceptional cases, the mother does not desire her own sex as object of pleasure, but rather the sex that is complementary to her own, that is, the man's).

The girl, as a non-Oedipal object for her mother, will feel that she is unsatisfactory, incapable of satisfying. This is the first of the consequences of her mother's non-desire: the girl – and later the woman – is never satisfied with what she has or what she is. She is always yearning for a body other than her own: she would like a different face, different breasts, different legs. Every woman, by her own account, has something about her body which does not look right.

For the first thing that did not look right was indeed something about the body, since it was about her sex not triggering desire in her mother. The little girl, in her mother's eyes, will be sweet, lovable, graceful, good – anything but sexually alive, tinged with desire. The colour of desire will not be found in the little girl that has been handled by a woman.

And yet, even at that time, her sex is a fact, and the vulvo–clitoral area is hypersensitive to the mother's touch when she cleans the child; but that sex is not an object of desire for the mother who, in line with the culture, does not see this part of herself as 'typically female', rather reserving that distinction for her vagina, which the man has pronounced 'fit for orgasm'. It is the mother, then, who first bars the way to her daughter's clitoral orgasm and institutes silence on the subject of that orgasm.

The 'thou art a clitoral child' is replaced by the 'thou shalt be a vaginal woman who will come to climax with a man – later on'. A present tense which is forbidden for the sake of a future which must be waited for: that, alas, is how it will be for a great many women, still caught up in the wait for the orgasm of the adult woman who, like the little girl, knows that there is a climax lying ahead but is never aware of one at the time. So the girl is denied in her own sexuality and told to wait for her future sexuality as a woman; she must keep to herself what she is (a clitoral child) and believe in what she is not (a vaginal woman).

Grasping the dialectic that is being imposed on her, guessing that only the woman is regarded as a sexual being, she plays at being a woman: she borrows the tricks of her trade: the lipstick, the high heels, the handbag. The little girls gets herself up as a woman, just as later on the woman will disguise herself to look like another woman, different from the one she is.

That is the origin of the permanent 'displacement' of the woman with respect to her own body: there's never any harm, in her view, in the odd bit of cheating if it means being accepted as a woman. Her real sex is not enough; she is always having to make more of it. And what do women's magazines go on about, if not the 'really natural woman', the 'womanly woman', the 'woman that *is* a woman', and so on? As if there always had to be something added to the woman's own sex, as if the woman were not woman by nature, as if her sex were not the signifier of her femininity. Surely all this is – once more, once again – the story of the little girl who has to show herself as sexed differently from how she actually is? And was it not right back in childhood that the woman first started to tell lies about her actual sex? There are no genuine little girls; there are only make-believe little women.

Everyone knows that to get yourself recognized as a girl, it is not enough just to be one: you have to be continually adding on proofs of femininity which, often, have nothing to do with sex.

> The boy is desired for his own sake . . . . The girl is desired – if and when she is so – according to a scale of values . . . :
>
> – girls are more loving . . . ,
>
> – they are more grateful . . . ,
>
> – they are sweet and charming . . . ,
>
> – they help about the house . . . .[12]

All in all, the girl is pronounced 'girl' for a thousand reasons which never have anything to do with her actual sex; she is given conditional recognition as 'girl', while the boy is recognized as boy entirely because of his sex. The girl always has to bring forward proofs of her femininity. Following on from that, how could women not be haunted by the need to put the signs of that femininity on public display? What a life it is for the woman who thinks she has to go on proving all her life long that she really is a woman! A woman – something even she is never wholly certain of being, since her social identity seems never to have stemmed from the sex of her body.

A painful dialogue in which *identification* (being like) matters more than *identity* (being oneself), in which *make-believe* replaces *genuine*. Identity blocked by lack of desire from the other sex, identification imperilled by the difficulty she has in seeing her own body as being like her mother's: these are the twin hazards that lie along the girl's road.

The little girl's trouble is that her body is not like anyone's. She possesses neither a sex like her father's nor the distinguishing features of her mother (who has breasts, comes in at the waist and out at the hips, has pubic hair). The little girl sees herself as naked, flat, and with a slit – something like the sexless dolls on sale in shops.

She does have something which really is 'like', but it is something she can't see, something hidden away inside her slit. And no-one ever tells her about this clitoris, the only sexual point of comparison with her mother.

For anyone who really wants to see some lightening of the darkness that surrounds women's sexuality, the clitoris – so much built up by feminists, so much played down by male chauvinists – may well be one of the earliest links that must not be bypassed in the developmental chain. For when the girl is not told about this part of her sexuality, what happens is that she is denied mention of what she has, and told instead, in general terms, about her as yet non-functioning genital endowment. She is told about what she does not have (periods, reproductive processes) and her mother does have.

And because of all this, the mother cannot be a locus of identification for the girl. Homosexual feelings between them are ruled out: only in adolescence will the girl discover that there are bodies like hers – hence the importance of friendship between girls in that period, setting up the femininity which could not be set up with the mother.

On the other hand, faced with this mother who is unlike her, who is better endowed than she is, the girl does discover envy and jealousy which do not – as Freud thought – stem from the relationship with the male body, but from the overwhelming comparison with that of the woman-and-mother.

It is not uncommon to see a little girl touching first her mother's breasts and then her own chest and saying 'Katie no boobs.' Long before the man's penis, is it not rather, in view of the mother's predominant presence, the sexual attributes of the mother that are felt as missing from the child's body? Creating in the boy the irreversible lack and enduring fantasy of the comforts of the maternal breast, and, in the girl, the endless comparing with and jealousy of any other breast (any other body) better shaped than her own?

In any case, if that is where women are stuck, and if jealousy has taken the place of homosexuality, it is because the mother, first and foremost of the women to be encountered, was unable to bring herself to recognize or name that part of her daughter's body which in fact is like part of hers. Out of shame? Out of fear? No woman ever talks to her daughter about the clitoris.

And so, in despair at having no sex (the clitoris unrecognized), and no sexual object (the father absent), the little girl will go on, not, as Freud thought, to repress her sexuality, but to displace a sexuality which, as such, is impossible.

If there is nothing sexual in her sex, there will be enough and to spare everywhere else. The girl sexualizes everything: her body, which has to be feminine, her acts, which have to be in line with those of her kind, her language, which becomes seductive. The woman will sexualize whatever can be seen by the other. Since her sex got no recognition when she was a little girl, the woman will contrive to get it for the other, unsexed parts of her body. With the result that sometimes she will take her whole body as a sexual signal and then will be afraid to display it; like the woman who said to me one day: 'When I have to get up and speak, and everyone can see me, I get confused about what I want to say, my mind goes blank. I'm overcome with shame, all I can think of is my body, and then I just don't know where to put myself.'

The woman learns in childhood to use her external features to signify her internal sex. The little girl spends her time giving external proofs of her femininity, which the adults round her keep a closely guarded secret, and, following on from that, she will stop being able to tell what is sexual about her and what is not.

It will be said of her that she becomes hysterical because she appeals continually to the gaze of the other to guarantee her sexual identity. What difference is there between her and the man, other than that the man is given this desiring gaze from the outset, by his mother? The absence of any paternal gaze in earliest childhood seems to register in the girl as sexual anxiety, as an identificatory doubt that has forever to be allayed, forever made good by the gaze of another in adulthood.

What woman can claim to be indifferent to the gaze that is directed at her? Whether it is perceived as conferring or as demolishing structure, the fact is that the woman finds great difficulty in moving outside the orbit of the gaze, and in especial the gaze of the man. This is the explanation of the difficulty, the ambivalence, that women feel over leaving the phallocratic world of the man for the world of the feminist woman who reckons as valueless the judgement of the man, and derives no prestige from his consideration.

Women are afraid that, if they do, they will lose something like the ability to 'attract' the man. Women do not trust other women in anything that has to do with recognition: they are afraid, when in the company of women, of finding themselves once again facing the rivalry they knew with the first woman of all, their mother. The war with the mother, with Jocasta, has ushered in the reign of mistrust rather than homosexuality. And women find it very hard to get through their mistrust of one another. The 'sisterhood' is not an obvious next step: it requires them to give up the pattern of existence they learn from outside and to take up instead the existence that comes from inside. And that is a very unfamiliar direction for a woman to move in.

In honour of women we shall have to alter Descartes' 'I think therefore I am' to read 'I attract therefore I am.' Which sets up between the physical and the moral a fundamental antinomy which is exclusive to women, as witness the dreaded anorexia in girls that comes about in adolescence when the signs of femininity become outward and visible and there is no getting away from attracting. Some girls experience the change as the surrender of their own identity to the identity conferred on them by the gaze of the 'other', and they are the ones who will do everything to elude this gaze, to hide these new features, which they see as their downfall.

The anorexic is 'her own woman', she refuses to be a woman 'for others', and so she will have nothing to do with the usual canons of beauty and femininity. She lives by norms of her own which allow her to elude desire. These girls reveal, through their frequently suicidal outlook, that the adolescent girl faces a basic choice between body and mind, for, oddly enough, these girls who so obviously refuse the body as site of alienation for the gaze of others present a much higher level of intellectual development than most of their classmates, who have gone over to the other side, the desirable women.

There can be many obstacles on the road to 'femininity' and psychoanalysts, while they may see very few little girls (for they are not yet caught in the body–mind dilemma and can live among the dreams and sublimations vouchsafed to them by the neutrality of their bodies), see a great many adolescents and women whose development has been stopped by the refusal to attract. They generally put the blame on their mother, finally identified as the source of their troubles, since she gave them only a place without a sex and they refuse the place of woman that is being pushed at them, too late, and even then conditional. The girl's Oedipal opposition (to desire from the opposite sex) cannot come out into the open until the actual encounter with masculine desire, until adolescence, therefore; but it can last a lifetime. The status of 'desired woman', because always acquired too late, will always be a locus of ambivalence among women, unless indeed it sets off open revolt, as recently with the emergence of feminism and the systematic refusal to submit to the desire of the 'desiring' male. Who, it seems, is totally taken aback: such violence from his partner amazes him, scandalizes him, for up till now he has never really grasped that the business of being a woman means giving up other kinds of success elsewhere, and that 'womanly women' are, intellectually speaking, so many 'underdeveloped areas'.

So it seems as if it might be because they have deliberately given up 'attracting' that women now are starting to talk, to write, to draw, to sing. How odd! Might there be, after all, an inverse relationship between 'attracting' and 'knowing', between woman-as-object and woman-as-mind? The social ideal might lie in the woman who can keep the delicate balance between these two.

The Oedipal trace

From this Oedipal relation, in which the father is so overshadowed by the mother, we all of us emerge bruised and battered, bearing the mark of our mother and dreaming of our father.

In the man, this takes the form of a resentment of women which no man ever gets over entirely or for good. Male identity is stamped with the refusal of the woman as equal. In the woman, it is more like a frantic chase after male desire, a chase which will make her bow to the law of the man and mistrust other women. Female identity is stamped with the desire to encounter the man who has so long been missing from her life.

Here then we can see the infernal circle taking shape in which the woman, undesired in childhood, goes begging as an adult for the desire and approval of the man, while he, given the master's role, will take advantage of the fact to get his own back on the woman (in memory of his failure to get his own back on his mother). And so the woman searching for the reparative love of a man will stumble into the castrating love of the man who has made up his mind that never again would 'she' be in command. It seems that what has been lived through with Jocasta will trigger both jealousy in women (over the conquest of the man), and misogyny in men. With the result that the woman finds herself viewed with distrust by both sexes; it will be hard indeed for her to avoid war.

And to think that what women are suffering under is something they brought on themselves by insisting on having sole charge of the child's upbringing! To think that it is mothers who train up the future misogynists who will make their daughters' lives a misery!

Are we, men and women alike, forewarned of all this? Apparently not, since women still seem to go in both for claiming the child as theirs and for needing to be 'recognized' by the adult male. Women cannot get out of the place men assign them to. This is what they are complaining of at present, without any idea that, for the man, this is the only way he can win the battle with his mother, first and foremost of the women in his life.

Whatever appearance the couple may take on, it is still the place where the woman wants to be 'recognized' by someone who cannot grant her 'recognition' without feeling endangered; which is why men are deaf to feminist grumbles, for all that these are often justified.

But it is not by mistaking conclusions for premises that women are going to be able to put right the wrongs that have been done to them; it is by changing the premises. Then they will produce men who, having been much less subject during childhood to the power of women, will feel far less need to defend themselves against that power when grown up.

It is the women who do the grumbling, because under the present system it is they who are the more oppressed. But they must realize that the more they ask to be given the care of the child (and not a day passes but the State suggests they should), the more they will perpetuate the phallocratic system that confines them. One sex must step back so that the other can take its place in the child's Oedipal configuration. Can women face giving away so much? Can men face taking on their share of Oedipal power?

5

Anatomy or destiny?

> for I
> Suffered those deeds more than I acted them,
> As I might show if it were fitting here
> To tell my father's and my mother's story . . .
> I had to face a thing most terrible,
> Not willed by me, I swear.
>> Sophocles, *Oedipus at Colonus*, in David
>> Grene and Richmond Lattimore (eds),
>> *The Complete Greek Tragedies* (3 vols,
>> Chicago, 1959), II, 91 ff

If there are radical differences between the sexes in the way they go through the Oedipal phase, it should be possible, by following the exact route a child takes between that phase and adulthood, to find markings that are specific to each sex.

It is important, therefore, that we look closely at the earlier stages of childhood, so as to know whether or not male and female children go through these in the same way.

What can we see of these stages? What can we know of them? What traces remain, in adult years, of this earliest face-to-face encounter with the mother? What does the man or the woman have to say about it when they talk to their analyst? And is the analyst not ideally placed to recognize, amid the words and thoughts of the adult, the trace of this primary relationship with the mother? Surely the analyst is one of the few people who can spot how far traces of the Oedipal phase are still present, even though the marks it has left on the man and the woman are very different. And if Freud, borrowing Napoleon's quip, could say 'anatomy is destiny', was there not a psychoanalyst to write recently: 'Anatomy is not really destiny. Destiny is what men make of anatomy.'?[1]

If Freud's main discovery lies in his proving that the adult's sexuality depends on the child's, his greatest failure is that he did not look closely enough into the question of how far the sex of the child interacts with the sex of the adult responsible for his or her up-bringing.

As we have seen, anatomy has a decisive role to play in establishing the earliest relation, and we know that that relation is the model for all subsequent relationships in the life of the individual. So everyone's future is connected with his or her anatomy, but above all with what the adult who undertakes the rearing makes of that anatomy.

And just what does this child-rearer do that is so different between the sexes? And what kind of response does the child make, right from the earliest moment? These are questions which must be put and answered through a close examination of the behaviour of girls and boys during the most primitive stages of infancy; the so-called pre-genital stages.

Oral stage and object relations

In the earliest moments of its life, the baby seems to live in the vegetative mode, as close as possible to intra-uterine life. It seeks above all to fill itself and to sleep. It is apparently unable to sleep unless it is full. This looks like a consequence of its long uterine existence, during which, sleeping for the most part, it lived a life in which it was filled and surrounded by the amniotic fluid in which it bathed. Its half-open mouth had as yet no awareness of 'emptiness', any more than did its alimentary canal, which has been shown to be operative *in utero*, with the child swallowing and digesting, since, when it is born, it excretes meconium, the contents of its intestine.

When it is born, then, the child has no knowledge of 'emptiness', and will try to fend it off by all possible means: stuffing its fist in its mouth, sucking the edge of its sheet – anything at all, as long as there is something in this mouth so accustomed to 'fullness'.

The ingesting of food does seem to be the ideal moment for the original continuity of inside and outside to be re-established, and it is the most intense moment of the infant's life. But even as it goes through the motions of sucking, it cannot fail to internalize, to fill itself with the whole maternal context surrounding the feed. The entire maternal *Gestalt* finds its way inside the baby: smell, warmth, tone of voice. The infant assimilates everything that comes from its mother (or whatever woman looks after it), for in this early phase it makes no distinction between its own 'person' and that of the 'other'. The baby, then, introjects far more than food; as proof we have the trauma of hospitalization where that is accompanied by the sudden absence of the woman who normally brings up the child. Even though all the familiar kinds of care are lavished on it, the child no longer knows where 'it' is, now that it has lost the maternal context that had made up its world. It seems to have lost a part of itself, and to be suffering from a loss which to all appearances is merely external.

Faced with feeding difficulties resulting from hospitalization, Françoise Dolto hit on the idea of wrapping the baby in, or placing on the bed, a piece of material that belongs to the mother and smells of her, which allows the child to feel itself back in the 'maternal set-up', and to start sucking again.

There would have been no point in following this roundabout path if it did not prove how dependent the child is, in its first few months, on the atmosphere created by the mother, and how this mother, according as she is more or less desiring, will establish the child as more or less loved, more or less desired.

The quality of parental love at this stage of life will entail the quality of self-love or *narcissism* that lies at the base of the self-confidence, the libidinal life-energy of the future adult.

The mother's behaviour, stemming from her unconscious feelings about the baby, will be the element that induces the particular behaviour pattern of this baby. When we go right back to this earliest, oral stage, what do we notice in mothers dealing with their children of different sex? Does the mother's behaviour vary with the sex of the child?

Girls are for the most part weaned earlier than boys.[2]

Mothers stop giving the bottle to girls, on average, in the twelfth month, and to boys in the fifteenth.[3]

The feed is longer for boys: at two months, forty-five minutes, against twenty-five minutes for girls.[4]

According to these scientific findings concerning very young children, it looks as if the mother does more for boys than for girls.

Feeding difficulties have been found in 94 of the girls in each group studied (slowness, vomiting, rapid changes of mood), but in only 40 of the boys. These features appear from the first month in 50 of the girls, who tend to have small appetites until the age of six, whereas difficulties of this kind appear late in boys and take the form of rapid changes of mood.[5]

So we see that the girl appears to run into trouble with the mother early on, earlier at any rate than the boy, and, if we follow it carefully, we can find in the lives of grown women the mark of this oral stage which they found so hard at the very start: is it not the case that anorexia, bulimia, and vomitings are female symptoms rather than male ones?

On the analyst's couch, the words women use to talk about being 'full' and 'empty' are no less indicative of oral difficulties experienced in the earliest relation with the mother. Here are some that go back to those days:

'I keep on *swallowing*, swallowing, I feel I'm swallowing everything my mother tells me. I have no defence against her or the horrible things she says. It's awful how much it hurts.'

'I *throw up* every day. I've always thrown up, ever since I was little – I eat and then I throw up, then I feel better, cleaned out, empty at last.'

'I bake cakes, big ones, giant ones. What really matters is for them to rise a lot so they'll be huge, so I can tell myself there's all anyone could want, all anyone could eat, so I won't have to *go without*.'

'Suddenly the feeling comes over me – I've got to eat, eat anything, anyhow. I've got to *fill myself up* until I can't eat another bite, then I feel ashamed. But all the time I'm stuffing I don't feel tense or worried: there's just me and the food.'

'I don't know what I say here, but I do know this, that I have a *good feed*. That's right, I feel like I get a feed. What of? The atmosphere in the room? You?'

'I'll never be able to pay you for all I *get from you*.'

'When you talk to me, I'm ever so pleased: *I drink in* your words, I get something inside me. Sometimes I notice that I don't even know what you said. All I've heard is the sound of you speaking.'

This is what seven women patients have to say, women utterly different in age, symptoms, position. Nothing, apparently, to connect them with one another, except this dramatically 'oral' hunger that comes in all sorts of guises, even that of vomiting for fear of having swallowed something bad. I have not picked up anything like this from men patients, for they have never told me anything comparable. It seems that 'oral' desperation is not for them, for they were given the perfect feed, in which desire added a special flavour to the milk that gave them sustenance. (The man will be located elsewhere, in the furious 'anal' defence of his person. We shall look for him later where we are sure to find him: in a fight.)

And so excess of 'emptiness' and desire for 'fullness' will take the woman into the kitchen where she will take up her position somewhere between the fridge and the cooker, by way of the sink. And when she is there, believe me, there is a general chorus of 'Hurrah' and praise for the lady on her orality. No-one will make any effort to point her in a different direction. On the contrary: she will be told that this is the place that has been planned for her since the dawn of time, that this is her kingdom, that her reign over her family world is assured. What a sham it is, what an infernal circle, in which mothers provide for whole families so that, by this round-about route, they can feed the hungry little girl they carry inside them!

By the mechanism of projection, each woman imagines that every-one else is like her and therefore famished, and, herself insatiable, feels obliged to feed them till they can eat no more. In the lives of women an unprotected, empty inside cohabits strangely with a generous outside.

Women, it seems, tend to mix up 'loving' and 'feeding'. Where do they get this odd internal equivalence from? Where if not the fact that they have always thought of themselves as not fed properly, because not loved properly by a mother who did not desire them? The bottle was empty since it did not taste of 'desire'. We are back once more with this bottle that is full of milk but empty of desire because it is given by a woman of the same sex as the girl.

From 'not fed properly' to 'not fucked properly' is no more than a step which, as we shall see, the woman takes blithely enough on her way to saying, on the subject of her night-time romps:

'His sex *frightens* me. I'm afraid that it will be too big. I feel threatened – I'm afraid of it going too far in and hurting me.'

'I really like the foreplay. I'd like it all to stay there, on the surface, because as soon as he gets inside me, I go tight and *it hurts*.'

'And then there's masturbation: I just don't know what happens. If I do it, it's fine, but if he does it, it hurts. I don't come. I *feel cross with him*, and it can't work like that.'

'He complains that I don't have any desire for him, that I never ask him for anything. But *I've never asked for anything*: not from my mother, not from anyone. I'm used to managing on my own. I don't need him.'

'I can't make love the way he wants – without saying anything, without cuddling. I need him to say things, to stroke me. I need to feel loved. I couldn't care less about the rest: that's just for him.'

All of which throws some light on frigidity as the refusal of what comes from the 'other' because it is equated with what came from a bad mother and seemed harmful and dangerous. The sex and the man it belongs to are surely being seen here as essentially 'bad'.

Oral frigidity is something often found in women who, from inability to take their man for a good mother, transfer on to him all their destructive fantasies, and can find no other recourse than analysis in the present for erasing their catastrophic past. One story can wipe out another, but it will be no easy matter for one image to take the place of another when that other is quite so deep-rooted, so ancient. It will be an uphill struggle, for if this woman started out by having a bad time sucking in opposition to her mother, then went on to have a bad time making love in opposition to her man, it will be a long time before she can persuade herself to get herself out of this in opposition to her analyst.

Yet for as long as this first relation with the mother has not been put right, there is no chance of her getting a second one right with anyone whatever. The heterosexuality which was missing from the little girl's life is often missing still from the life of the woman.

Along the road between cradle and wedding-night we shall often find marks showing anorexia as a girl (refusal to feed herself, to fill herself), or bulimia (excessive need to eat in order not to feel empty). All these symptoms, which we found women typically more disposed to, indicate a conflict-ridden relationship with food which may surface in many forms. There is no equivalent in men that has a frequency to match this, in childhood, in adolescence, or in adult life.

The emergence of language

The beginnings of communication in the infant can be put at about 10 or 12 months. This age immediately follows the mirror stage (7–8 months) during which the child finally achieves differentiation from the mother and moves on definitively from symbiosis with her. Seeing her at the same time as itself in a mirror or window, it discovers that there are two of them, that 'it' is not 'she'; that it is separate and independent of her. The child turns its face towards the woman who is holding it in her arms, touches her nose and realizes that this is not-it. Never again, outside psychosis, will the child return to the 'all' with the mother.

Once the child has become aware of being separate, it will have much more marked reactions to the absence of its mother or the woman who looks after it. It cries when laid back in the cot, and cries again to be picked up. The child develops shifts of mood and learns to put into its screams its insistent appeal to the other. If at the start of its life the baby cries from physical discomfort or hunger, from the mirror stage onwards it learns to cry because of the absence of its mother, an absence experienced as something missing, as a lack. Speech soon follows in the form of onomatopoeic noises which become more and more precise and codified by the family world. Then the child will learn to indicate desire by means of words.

Thus, starting out from the cry, signal of physical discomfort, the child rapidly reaches the highest level of communication: language.

Here too we find obvious disparity between the sexes, for the girl will talk far sooner than the boy of the same age and 'intellectual' level. This fact is taken to be the norm in all treatises on infancy. But must we really accept this without further question? What does it stem from?

If the function of the baby's appeals and cries is to indicate perception of separation from the mother and to restore connection with her, it appears that girls, having cried more during their first months, start to talk earlier. Which points to an *absence*, a distance to be travelled in order to get back to the mother; no such absence or distance exist for the boy of the same age.

For the boy is not driven by intense anxiety about being left alone: that is a condition he has no experience of, since from the moment of birth he is sustained by the maternal fantasy of wholeness, which makes of him a narcissistic object; he is happy where he is, as he is.

If, then, the girl talks earlier, it is because she does not bathe in the same comfort. She has no-one for whom she is complementary, since it is not as a general rule her father who is her nurse. She talks earlier because she feels she is alone and is intent on restoring a link with her mother. This link will not be felt as internal, so she must talk, in order to receive an external response. This will make up to some extent for her lack of inner narcissistic image.

Already we can see forming, in earliest childhood, the differences that will mark the language of the man and that of the woman. One language begins early and functions as maker of connections, as that which can cancel the unbearable distance from other people. This is women's language: leaving no gaps, on the look-out for similarities, seeking assent (which, as coming from the father, the little girl has always lacked). Women are often said to be too much inclined to tell their life-stories. The other language, starting late, is the very embodiment of the distance at which other people must be kept. Men's language is commonly devoid of feeling, good or bad. The man keeps to safe, non-committal generalities. As we know so well, he is not out looking for intimate connections: of those, it seems, he has had enough with his mother to do him for the rest of his life. But we shall return to the vexed question of male and female speech. It merits proper discussion – and an explanation that goes beyond saying that neither side wants to understand the other. For the moment let us simply note that the girl's early access to language is not necessarily a sign of desirable development. Haste, after all, has never been a sign of self-confidence; far from it!

Then again, might not what women themselves say settle the matter?:

'If I stop talking I'm afraid that you'll see that I don't amount to anything.'

'I talk, I'm noisy, but inside, I'm afraid. It's all empty.'

'If I let the silence take over again, I won't be able to bridge the distance between us. It frightens me.'

Whereas from the men we hear:

'I don't know what I'm doing here. I haven't anything to tell you. There's nothing I feel like sharing with you.'

'Got to keep quiet so as to keep a distance. I hate talking when we make love. I don't want to bring feeling into it – I hate the closeness my wife is looking for.'

'How can I manage so 'she' won't know? Impossible. Even if I don't say anything, she guesses. I could go to the other end of the world and she'd still know everything about me. It's terrible to have something stuck to you like that.'

Radical difference between the man's need and the woman's: a difference that is located in distance – what the man fights to get and keep, what the woman must at any cost avoid. This is the language-mark that Jocasta has left on each one of us.

Father who, here too, would have been indispensable, for his son just as much as for his daughter, for he would have restored the balance by his closeness to the daughter, his distance from the son.

Mothering by the father: the vital need for this has never been set out properly, whereas mothering by the mother fills columns beyond counting in publications of every kind!

Anal stage and basic ambivalence

Pursuing our investigation through the different stages that make up infancy, we quite naturally come on now to the anal stage. During this, the auto-erotic pleasure of expelling or retaining the faeces has to give way before the desire for cleanness of the adult in whose care the child is; the shift from private pleasure to the need to make offerings.

Merciless battle between adult demand and the child's response. Sacrifice of its own law to the law of the other, recognized as social obligation; the first of the frustrations that have to be accepted in order to be one of the 'grown-ups'.

The child has enormous ambivalence about this gift that is required of it. At the outset there is the fear that if it hands over its excreta it will be handing over its whole self and thereby vanishing altogether. Hence those anal games in which we can see the child absorbed in alternately filling and emptying some tiny container. It will stare at the water running away, then it will watch carefully as it rights the beaker again. It will observe that its beaker is still there in its hand, although the water has gone. This is how it learns the permanence of the container; for in all this fuss it has got into with its mother over cleanness, the child itself is the container. What the mother is demanding is the contents.

There before us is the child, already able to symbolize. It has only a little way to go before it can sublimate. For that, in the end, is its escape route. Sublimation will allow it to get back to anal pleasures, now in guises which are viewed more favourably, indeed positively encouraged by adults. This is the age of mess: games with earth, sand, water – all of them things which, unlike excreta, the child will be provided with. It is the age too when we see the child going about with arms overloaded with objects. If one thing falls, the child gets upset, stops, puts all the other things down so as to pick up the first one. Everything the child does points to the care it is taking not to lose anything – a form of compensation for the fact that it 'loses' its excreta.

Here once again a surprising fact: girls are clean sooner than boys. Obviously this too is an area where maternal conditioning can be seen at work by anyone who cares to look: 'Mothers are more easygoing with boys, even when they dirty their pants (it is well known that boys are less clean than girls even when they are older), but girls are expected to be cleaner.'[6]

In another finding, Brunet and Lézine report:

Difficulties in toilet training occur earlier in girls and last less long (between the ages of fifteen and eighteen months for girls, between twenty-four months and four years for boys) because in boys they take the form of sullen and prolonged opposition, accompanied by interminable rituals.[7]

No doubt about it: the anal battle is boys' business – opposition is men's business. It looks as if, in this respect, the girl has moved ahead of the boy; as if, by managing to get through the 'solitude' of the mirror stage early, she has been quicker to reach language and its symbolization, which will help her to realize that she can let 'it' go and yet keep all the rest of herself intact. This is a notion which the boy finds hard to take in because at that age he is still so much caught up in the symbiotic relation with his mother. Moreover, hysterical reversal is taking hold in the girl more and more markedly. She finds herself obliged to provide proofs of her femininity – this proof, any proof – whereas the boy is still back in earlier territory; it will be hard indeed for him not to feel in danger of being sucked back in by the mother and her desire.

And he has the vague feeling that it is his sex that makes his mother particularly attached to him. He thinks she is after his sex as well as his excreta. He believes she wants to get it away from him, cut it off, steal his strength as a boy, goodness knows what else. Freud called this 'castration anxiety', and 'they' call women 'castrating'.

At all events, in the anal stage panic sets in for the little boy: he holds out, he refuses, he delays, for he thinks that they're not just out to get his stool, they're out to get him. He starts to wet and soil himself and his bed – these are male symptoms far more often than female. He wants no part of what 'she' is asking from him; he sees himself as got at, directly affected, threatened (castrated?).

If and when he relives that same fantasy in later years, he becomes impotent or suffers from premature or delayed ejaculation. He will not want – will not be able – to give 'her' what 'she' wants; a burdensome consequence of the war waged by son against mother.

This is where the struggle with woman starts. This is where the misogyny that women so frequently complain of first appears. What they do not know is that it all goes back to another woman who also clung to her privilege as mother, and implanted in her son the unconquerable fear of castration whenever and wherever female desire appears.

In the anal stage, the boy plays war. He takes his soldiers and invents enemies and friends, imagines winners. He threatens, he kills; all of which, transposed, is what he feels. He is at war with his mother over something which was originally his (his stool) but which she is now trying to get away from him. But then, maybe winning this war, by refusing to fall in with the desire of the mother, might be too dangerous. Might he not run the risk of losing the woman he loves? Here is the source of his ambivalence towards women. A man will spend his time knocking the woman off her throne in one place and crowning her Queen somewhere else. Can he live without 'adoring' this woman over whom, in other respects, his phallocratic empire gives him sway? Here, then, misogyny and ambivalence stand for the first time together; from now on they will move as one within the man.

In any case, during his long anal resistance to his mother, the man, it would seem, has learned how best to insure against attack from without – something which will stand him in good stead, not only in his marriage but beyond. Will he not be an unyielding defender of his rights, his goods and chattels, his freedom?

And was it not with his mother, felt as 'castrating', that he first began to defend himself so forcefully, so aggressively as soon as anyone laid hands on what was his? First he experienced the struggle against symbiosis with her; now comes the struggle against her express desires. Because of all this, the man goes on smarting at the memory that someone tried to cut off first his sex, then heaven knows what. Because of this he has developed the habit of steering clear of appeals, holding back, keeping his counsel, giving nothing away so as not to run into the danger of coming off worst. All this reappears in analysis. Listen now to what gets said on the couch:

'I'm not going to say a thing, just to make it hard for you. So there. I've every right to keep quiet – I've paid for it.'

'I've come into analysis because I know you have to be silent. You're caught. My mother always had to get her word in . . . Bloody hell.'

'I can't bear it when you talk. I feel trapped. It's as if you were in my way.'

'Analysis with a woman? It's about seeing which of us comes out on top.'

'Speech as distance, speech as a wall, as a protection, to act as a rampart to prevent the other from coming closer.'

'It's not having to pay that I mind. What I can't stand is you enjoying money that's mine. I can't bear it that I'm giving you something.'

'Not remembering dreams so as not to be nice to the analyst.'

'. . . . .'

The last one said nothing at all. He at least can be sure that he left nothing behind him.

The man's obsession: to give me nothing, to place me as a woman who is dead, non-existent; to fight against me for years and years so as to win against me. Is this not the exact reverse of what we heard a moment ago from the women who came to see me so that they could get a feed, take something away, pay, and so on? Negative, aggressive words I most often hear from men, seldom from women (it does happen, exceptionally, that a woman was treated as a sexual object by her mother).

The man's anal game comes down to this: how to stop the other from existing; how to remove all trace of her desire; how to kill her in fantasy. These murderous wishes come back into play each time man confronts woman, and especially 'his' woman. He comes to me complaining that his wife is asking for things that upset him, things that seem somehow particular to her. Sexuality for him is the ground of his revenge, his sovereignty, whereas what he is complaining about is that she wants to get something out of it for her. His complaint is that she has a desire of her own. He finds it outrageous that she should want to exist at all differently from how he has willed it.

But let us rather listen in again:

'When we're making love, I don't like her to move or say anything. That turns me right off.'

'I can only make it with my wife if I feel a bit remote from her. Otherwise I can't.'

'What I'd really like would be to screw some woman I knew nothing about, somebody who wouldn't be asking for anything. Above all, no intimacy, no sharing: just the body.'

'Sex = revenge = rape. There you are. It's dead simple: screw as many of them as possible, so I can get my own back as much as possible.'

'After we've made love, she'd like me just to lie beside her, but I can't. I go all funny inside. It's a bloody horrible feeling. I've got to get rid of it right away – eat or drink something, get something inside me.'

'She'd want me to be whispering sweet nothings in her ear. I just can't, because I have to have this distance from her. She'd like me to be really close.'

Does it not look, from these snatches lifted from a long litany of male grievances, as if men are obsessed with Distance, Silence, Loss? Even when a man wants coitus with the woman he loves, is he not most of all afraid of *fusion* with her?

Here surely, at the very heart of sexual relations, we are once again faced with the anal dialectic: finding a way to give and yet hold the 'self' back, guard the 'self' against the other and her demands. When he does get into bed with her, is he not trying his best, most of the time, only to let his sperm go, and nothing else? The way the man sees it, he can use any technique, so long as it means giving nothing away. Is this what women expect from their partners? Unless and until men learn a whole new way of thinking, that is, until they are less afraid of what women may ask for, what kind of lovers are they going to make? When women are obsessed with closeness, intimacy, what kind of response are they going to get from men?

What the couch tells

In all this, the couch has operated as a magnifying glass, for the people we get coming to it are those men or women who have the outsize version of symptoms we expect to find in individuals described as 'normal'. What I as an analyst hear is what women manage to get said, although most women never say it; what men feel, although most men have achieved a near-perfect score for insensitivity.

What each of these patients has said, each one of us, man or woman, can echo: the patients put into words the complaint we call 'sexism'. They have been the dancers in a choreography where every step is precisely planned, and where men and women move in radically different ways. The word-ballet has been flawless: what he says, what she says (give or take a few turncoats) could be ascribed blindfold to the appropriate sex. We who are the children of Oedipus and Jocasta need no eyes to make our moves; the authentic message is written in our heart of hearts.

That is why Oedipus put his eyes out. But it was already too late. He had seen too much to forget. And so, not infrequently, have we
. . . .

6

A childhood memory

The road becomes easier as you go along, that is to say that if you keep on being obedient, meek and good, you become so accustomed to obeying that it no longer calls for effort.

Comtesse de Ségur[1]

Getting up in the night, when everyone is asleep, when my life is clear of other people, facing my own questions about the little girl that I once was; the girl who is so much like the ones I get told about on the couch. What is it that brings that little girl close to all those others? Silence: you and I have lived through the same silence, the conspiracy of silence that lies round our sex.

And I laugh when I think of the high excitement that came over me the moment my parents went out, leaving me by myself for a few hours. I would ransack the place – no, that's not it: I would carry out a systematic search of the drawer – and not just any drawer – *her* chest of drawers. The top drawer was boring: just letters, things kept for sentimental reasons, a few faded and yellowing photographs. No, what interested me was the second drawer, the one where she kept her underthings: bras, knickers, the sanitary towels that had me making all sorts of guesses . . . though not about sex, on the whole. When a little girl is told nothing about sex, what she wants to know about is the difference between her and her mother. She may have no idea where to locate this difference, but it's just got to be in the body somewhere. . . . And so, always despairingly, I would make my way to the drawer where my mother kept her underwear.

I should say that I had good reason to be intrigued, to have my suspicions that there was something going on that was being hidden from me. Not only was I aware of my father's attention to my mother, but only recently, when I was 6, she contrived to stagger me by telling me that I was going to have a little sister or a little brother. The origin of either was unguessable. I'm fairly sure that it was from then on that I started trying to find out my mother's 'secret'.

I don't think that any mother now would keep her child in ignorance, but the answers that mothers do give are as varied as political loyalties, and, believe me, this is not an area where the left does particularly well! All the way from the timeworn explanation about the baby sleeping in its mother's tummy (why sleeping, since it moves? Why in her tummy, unless because that diverts attention a while longer from a place further down: the lower belly, so close to the sex), to the rather frightening one about the doctor opening up the belly to look for the baby; I get the lot. It might be asked why so few women have the courage (is that what it is?) to tell the exact truth. The only answer there is, the only answer there can be, is that the 'secret' has to be kept – the one which so obviously bars the way to finding out about the vagina, and, perhaps, masturbation. Whereas all that is automatic in boys, over the little girl's sex there still hangs a cloud of mystery which is useful for making sure she goes on being a little angel. Well, at any rate, as you have just seen, an angel 'of sorts', who plays doctors and puts in the rectal thermometer – for the sensations that that brings are by no means negligible since, as you know, the anus and the vagina share the same muscles. But the orgasmic pleasure that goes on in that area may not come to the parents' attention. Then again, the 'little angel' may just as readily take to combing through other people's things, but is very unlikely to make sense of them.

Apart, then, from these occasional bursts of feverish investigation, I was the good little girl that I needed to be if I was to be liked and accepted by grown-ups. In actual fact, I felt they largely dismissed me. I was 'a child'; above all I was not a little woman, with the result that I couldn't see much of a connection between what I was and what I would become. And as to how I was actually going to become it, there were no answers there either: all blank, unknown, unknowable. The message was that I had to wait, and that I mustn't wish for what other people had – particularly not for what my mother had.

And yet one day, by an oversight, she forgot what she ought never to have forgotten, considering the care she took over my innocence;

there, lying in the lavatory bowl, I saw 'the thing', stained red with fresh blood. But what sort of thing was it? My thoughts (God preserve anyone acquainted so young with psychoanalytic fantasy) were of a shameful disease or a secret wound. I was never 'in' on what was happening in that house, especially not with my mother, so once again repression, once again the decision never to ask 'them' about anything ever again, not to see what I wasn't supposed to. After that it's easy to say that women are given to phobias, that is, are afraid to see or to know. Hence, it appears, the difficulties they have in ever seeing the whole picture – so much so that when they are driving they behave as if everything were immediate: braking too late and so on.

But let us pick up again the thread of my tiny existence – tiny up till then, at least. For if I had thought of myself as a sexless child uninvolved with her own body, my peace was to be shattered on the rock of my mother's words, when she told me that I was about to become a 'young woman' and have a discharge every month. This discharge my mother linked in a very scientific way with my secret opening and its future motherly and wifely function; but she said no word about desire, or pleasure. The whole thing struck me as impossible to accept; most of all I immediately connected it with the 'secret' which could have no other origin than the shame adults felt at doing such things.

So I acquired first breasts, then periods: glaring proof that I was part of the dreaded secret. There on my body were all these signs that I thought belonged to me; and what if 'they' didn't go and take them over? I shall never forget that cousin (whom I had never heard mention sexual matters, and who indeed never spoke of them again, except in the way of remarking on the good points of this lady or that) saying to my mother, as naturally as if he had just found out that the price of fruit had gone up: 'Well, well – Christiane is filling out', as he peered unambiguously at my new curves.

I wished the earth could have opened and swallowed me as I felt myself caught for the very first time by and in the appraising gaze of a man. Oh cousin, cousin, please don't mind now if I tell you that I wished you would be struck blind there and then! Had anyone ever asked you, even once in your life: 'Well then, Xavier my boy, had any wet dreams lately?' Of course they hadn't.

That day I became someone who would be looked at; first taken in at a glance, then taken to bed, then taken to wife, taken so that I might reproduce, and so on and so on. What a grisly nightmare: I was up for sale, for immediate occupancy: I would be the property of, the wife of, the mother of; I would *be* – but only if I took on those roles. Otherwise I would be nothing at all, I would just go on waiting.

Take it or leave it. But I was obstinate. I pretended not to understand. If a boy showed me he was keen on me, I would look as if I'd never heard the like, and tell him he was out of his mind or sex-mad. If another one asked me in all seriousness to marry him, I felt I'd been given a present of fools' gold, and shot off smartly. In short, I carried on like the typical bluestocking. I marvel today at an innocence that could hold out for so long, in a girl reckoned normal in other respects, that is, one whose appearance was as you'd expect, given her social class and educational attainments.

But this was all show, even if it fooled all and sundry. In actual fact, sickened at what was expected of me, I had set myself a very different target: to do really well at school and university. And, ignoring boys, that is just what I did.

I was absolutely set on being valued for my inner features, not my outward and visible ones. But alas, I had the sense that I was swimming against the tide, going against the grain. I was the only one who thought my scheme was working. Other people were only aware of my looks. How long was this farce going to go on?

I know now the answer to that question: *my whole life*.

In those days, I had to put up with wolf-whistles, propositions, comments on my charms – the sort of things that would put you off venturing out of doors. (Do you realize that there are a great many women who can no longer face going out in the street because out there they don't feel they're real people, just objects on display? Do you know that the first thing that strikes foreign girls when they come here is that women walking along the street will always be looking down or up, while the men look at them as and when they please?) What I used to hear was: 'I fancy you, I'd like to marry you, how about having a baby?' I could make no sense of what I heard – I knew that I was attractive to men on account of what mattered least in me. What I would have wanted was for someone to start from somewhere else – to talk about anything but externals. What I longed for was for someone to ask 'Who are you? What kind of thoughts have you got? What is your life like? What are you searching for?'

What I longed for was someone who would start out from some

ordinary human point that had to do with me, not with my wretched body which always seemed to get in the way; this body that brought me unwanted desire, this body that was always being compared with other girls', my friends' – this damned stupid body which, I at long last realized, was going to be my ally in the struggle for existence. God knows I wanted to exist, to live; but not that way!

And so, in the end, faced with 'their' single-mindedness, I made up my mind to use this thing that had market value for them and none for me. I started making use of this permanent injustice – for that is what beauty is. One smile and everything falls into place. All it took was for me not to hold out; in other words, I just had to shut up and let them look at me.

I was gradually discovering that, where I thought there was a fertile mind, what I had was a desirable body that men longed to take over, temporarily or permanently. I was beginning to see clearly that there would be little choice about what I would be fertile in; it would be babies. It was my good luck that I *could* give birth, for when women can't, they run into a different kind of unhappiness. When a couple can't have children, the man can recover by producing elsewhere. He will be able to make his mark in a different way. There is nowhere for a woman to make her mark, apart from the children she has. Imagine requiring all men to go into the same line of business!

For women there is only one business: love-making and child-bearing. For men there are hundreds, to suit all tastes, all gifts. Men can choose what they produce; women can not. They are bound to the fruitfulness of their womb.

To put it at its starkest: each member of the couple confines the other within a different set of problems: the wife is a prisoner of the husband's money, and the husband is a prisoner of the child that his wife will or will not give him. What a business!

And so: men and women live in the same building, but not on the same floor; and the segregation is absolute – rare indeed are those who change camp. Maternity and beauty are what make up the criteria for this segregation – you'd almost think that we women have done so well out of these two that we're happy to give up everything else. But who says we have? Men, no doubt eaten up by jealousy, stricken by the women's disease (envy for this or that), extracting life-long revenge by shutting us away in this whole wretched world of motherhood where they have no share. They readily grant us omnipotence in that world, while keeping every other kind of omnipotence for themselves. And yet have they not been fighting for years to retain control over this motherhood? Are we not used to seeing them lay into us about this future child which they saw as their choice, not ours? Their sovereignty over motherhood might be at one remove, but sovereignty is what it is. How could they ever have agreed to let go of the little that they could control directly, when it came to abortion on demand?

So it is that I live on the floor marked 'women', and, even though I got married (very late on), had children, fed husband and children, I never stopped reflecting on what had happened to me just because I had been born with a woman's sex. I thought about it long and hard, like other women, and, like them, I kept my thoughts to myself. The talk was less about my body than about my children, who were compared to other people's children. The same little game all over again; but now it was being played with our children. All women play at coming out on top with their children – who have no peace left, and find themselves caught up straightaway in competitiveness between women. And what joy are our little treasures supposed to get out of that?

My body had been the locus of norms and comparisons; now my children were to become trump cards in the fierce competition into which my birth had pushed me. But what competition? Was my life some card game where not all trumps counted? And by now it was clear that trumps wouldn't be the same for men and women.

So I decided to tot up the point count for the two of us. It didn't take long. Mine were all body points. His were for mind.

It was obvious that between the two of us we amounted to a 'complete whole' – provided I kept my thoughts to myself, and didn't want anything more in the way of femininity and maternity than . . . he saw fit to allow me.

If and when I look at my life as a child, if I look at my life as an adult – they pretty well coincide in any case – what do I see? I am being 'kept out'. I have to stay away from any social action that doesn't have to do with the body. If there is a woman in a ministerial post, it will be in Health, or Education, or Welfare. Women are kept at a safe distance – like witches, you can hear some of them saying.

7

The featureless desert

White sheets in a cupboard
Red sheets on a bed
Jacques Prévert,
Paroles (Paris, 1949)

What name can we give to that phase where little girls reign: the time when our daughters, all charm and conquest, are vainly searching for a partner who 'wants' them?

They are quick to leave their mothers' skirts, realizing that there is no rescue to be hoped for from that quarter. But where are they to go? Now the father, the alternative pole in the sexuality of the parental couple, has his turn at being sought after as the one who can appreciate what his daughter has and he hasn't: that hint of femininity which he can sense behind the little girl's curveless body. The girl yearns to be perceived as 'other', as different from the male sex; only the father can do this for her.

A little girl who has managed to get her father to put down his newspaper, has climbed up on his lap, is a little girl whose whole body attests that she has reached the place where for her all anxiety falls away. For the girl, the father is the way out of the absurd, the way into accepting her girl's body as 'good'. Her father is her goal.

But the father, alas, is not there for the most part. He is not at home, he is out all day, he will not be back till evening, and then only to talk to, go to bed with the mother. The little girl only comes alive through her mother's 'recorded broadcast'. The girl feels the despair of having no-one in whose eyes she exists; everyone loves her, but no-one thinks of her as having a sex. Her life is as flat as her body . . . Then she has an idea: since she can't have a real existence, she will devise one with her doll (what a good thing that the doll was invented; not so that girls can be conditioned to their future role as mothers, but because it is the only body-image that matches the little girl's). She has slipped quietly out from between the adults and gone off and found her like: a creature that can be just the same as she is, lacking only speech – which she will give her. Speech: the indispensable catharsis in the desert of loneliness that the girl-child must make her way through.

If you don't give a little girl a doll, she will make her own out of whatever is to hand or indeed hidden away inside herself, so that there shall be someone to talk to, if things go badly wrong. And there will be no shortage of things going badly wrong along *her* way! This doll of hers will be put through the girl's experience – her whole future, so long in coming, and at the same time her whole present as little girl who is 'unsatisfying' and therefore 'bad'. Have you ever noticed that in girls' play with dolls you always find the same two characters: the daughter and the mother? And that the daughter isn't good, and gets scolded by the mother? But what is this 'bad' doll if not the image of the girl herself? The good girl is the mother, with all her strengths as adult, sexually endowed and with access to the father's desire. For a little girl's life can only be lived in the *future tense*, as woman-to-be; the present is made up of non-existent sex and absent father.

Sometimes the little girl feels a longing to switch to the sexed body of a boy, who does at least have a genuine place. At these times, it is not the boy's penis that is the object of envy, but his actual status. Often girls want only boy dolls: either to scold them, or to make much of them because they have a place that the girl knows she can't have.

The girl has no way of getting past the barrier that could allow her through to the field of Oedipal desire. She has neither sexual strengths, since her sex is not recognized, nor sexual object, since her father (rare cases apart) is not the one who looks after her. Moreover, she is only familiar with half of her genitalia, her mother taking great care to avoid manually stimulating the other part. The mother will never set going anything but external clitoral masturbation (and even then she won't do it well, since she will not recognize her girl-baby's pleasure in this area because in most cases she doesn't recognize her own clitoris as typically feminine). And yet this primary, clitoral masturbation is and remains written into the girl's body, unaffected by any frigidity. This is something women know and will say, even if they feel a sort of shame in talking about it ever since Freud 'untalked' about it.

As far as the other half of her sex is concerned, she will be told (if she is lucky enough to be told anything) that it is for the man to unveil it for her when she's grown up. Always this future tense, always this man for whom she must wait and from whom revelation will come. Revelation of whom? Of what? Of his sexual pleasure? Of hers? The vagina, locus of pleasure common to man and woman? Locus symbioticus, psychoticus? Vagina, alienated, made over to the other, to the desire of the other, to the sexual pleasure of the other. Clitoris, clitoral orgasm; enjoyed away from the other; more genuine, perhaps, less suspect of play-acting. All questions that must be put whenever there is talk of the woman's double orgasm.

The whole point is that being a girl means living in anticipation. Psychically, it means hoping for the arrival of the man as adequate sexual object; physically, it means watching and waiting for the manifest proofs of a sex which has long been invisible.

But in the meantime, how can girls not yet sexually defined live except by imitating women? They will borrow the high heels, start using the make-up, even ape the way of talking: they will 'play grown-up ladies', since little girls have nothing worthwhile of their own, for value belongs exclusively to the 'ladies'. Nothing left for the little girl but imitation, given how she is kept out of everything; and all the time that her identity is surrounded by silence and secrecy, her identification is there for all to see – and to encourage: 'Doesn't she make a good mummy?'; 'What a good baby you've got.' It appears that among certain black tribes the element of pretence is even more marked: the little girl goes about with her belly sticking out and the women walking past pat it and say: 'Are you expecting, then?'[1] The mystification comes from outside: little girls are pushed into being women.

Rather than recognize what she has as specific to her as a little girl, people will nudge her on towards the beauty that lies ahead, the motherhood that will fulfil her, the marriage that will order her life.

In the earliest stage, she will be stopped from living to the full her sexuality as a little girl so that she can be a 'little angel'. What does an angel do? It lives 'up there', away up there in heaven, spiritually and only spiritually; so it is to sublimation that we must look in order to find the little girl. This sublimation which women are supposedly so short of is incredibly present and active in the life of little girls: girls draw better, write better poems, make up far livelier plays than boys.

However, come the second stage, they will be given instruction (above all round the time of puberty) in the cult of the body-as-attraction and of maternity as aim. Once they become women, girls will have a new objective, and will lose interest in sublimation.

Well, what else do you expect? It's not talk that the man wants from his wife (he has had enough of that from his mother): what he wants is for her to get her sexual pleasure 'from him', to have her children 'by him'. He is not interested in any sublimation his wife might go in for. The only one that is allowed, encouraged, is the one concerned with the educational sciences, with psychology (maybe even psychoanalysis: who can tell? Women are so good at everything to do with early stages). All the 'first steps' of human life are made over to her: in all their naturalness (these are things the body was made for); in all their castrating power for her herself. In the end, this sublimation, in Freud's view non-existent in women, makes me think not so much of female inability as of male prohibition. Man snatches sublimation away from woman by loading children on to her. Children who will be on her mind as long as she lives; a privilege that becomes a frustration. And no question of her putting in her oar elsewhere: 'elsewhere' is men: ideas, politics, science, industry. In short, the nation's brain-power. As for us, we must keep to bodies: bodies that are for orgasm, bodies that give birth, bodies that fall ill. That is where men want us to stay.

From adolescence on, following the encounter with the man, sublimation switches over; women are shut away in their bodies. It is a complete reversal of values: after ten or twenty years in a body that is sexless, she must serve thirty locked up in this fully-sexed body which arouses the interest of the other – that other whom she has so longed for! Now he is here, and, all against expectation, it is not life that he brings but death. She will carry on existing as a body, but in anything to do with the mind, she will be finished, or at any rate disabled.

It might be worth pausing for a moment on the life-style that the man has in mind for us. I open any women's magazine and am at once aware of the walls of my prison: the body and how to keep it young, cooking and how to be good at it, children and how to bring them up. I turn the pages, I look right through, I wait. What? Is that all there is? Yes: that is the woman's world. I am the prisoner of my own body and the slave of other people's.

A woman's body is a nuisance from start to finish: not there enough in the first stage, too much there later on, taking up the whole space of the woman's life. And women do not feel able to shake off the labelling of 'over-feminine' and 'under-feminine' that they get. Their whole lives are spent tacking helplessly this way and that between 'over' and 'under'. Often it's the 'under' that wins; often the body feels like the underside of the mind. Things I hear on the couch:

'If anyone looks at me, if a man takes any notice of me, I go all stupid: incapable of having thoughts, or making any kind of response, even to what he is actually saying.'

'I blow about like a leaf in the wind. Well, you see, a leaf doesn't have any depth or solidity.'

'My childhood? Nothing, nothing at all. I see it like a kind of total blank, an empty universe.'

'I can't get back any picture of me as a little girl. I think there was nowhere for me to be. I can remember my brothers, my mother, but as for me . . .'

As a woman, I could hardly fail to grasp what is being said, or understand that what all this points to is the impossibility of reaching any level of existence beyond that of outward appearance. I could hardly fail to remember that since, by way of inner world, the little girl had had to make do with outward appearances, what the woman is now demonstrating is that her inadequate looks go with an empty inner world. Or see that this emptiness experienced so often is the same one that marked the whole mother–daughter relationship from which desire was missing.

To live undesired is not to live at all: that, surely, is what we are being told by all those anorexic girls who, refusing desire, move on from there towards death. Why should they refuse desire, if not because it bursts without warning into the life of a girl utterly unfamiliar with it; familiar only with blank, sexless relationships with men and women alike. A woman's life is a colourless, featureless desert, then a brightly-coloured oasis, then once more the featureless desert. It is very hard for women to come to terms with so many brutal changes in their bodies; changes which take them from under to over and back again.

What a woman, every woman, longs for is to stay as long as possible in the brightly-coloured bit of her life. Her great fear is of going back to the 'blankness', the featurelessness of childhood. So that women, on account of their history, will make every effort to stay in the brightly-coloured 'Oedipal' position; which sets them firmly within the desire of men, who like their women dominated. Then the phallocratic song of the man will work like the sirens' song, drawing women to their destruction.

We have seen the price women have to pay in order to stay in the oasis. And then there are the intra-sex battles over the man that makes his entry, too late, into the life of the girl. These battles take the form of jealousies: the famous jealousy that first took hold in the presence of the overwhelming mother-and-rival, and which women must go through again with any and every female rival, seen as mortal enemy. If the boy, in his Oedipal history, resents first of all his father-and-rival, and then his possessive mother, the girl, for her part, resents only her mother, and then, after her, all other women.

'Women hate themselves', writes Annie Leclerc; but they hate themselves in the name of the mother who is too much present, and on account of the father, too much and too often absent from their lives as children, and whom, in consequence, they never want to leave.[2] It is striking to see how far the majority of women go in idealizing the father, in comparison with the very bad image they have of the mother – whatever the actual father may have been like. And if, for some glaringly obvious reason, the father cannot be built up, his daughter develops depressive or suicidal tendencies, for she is without any guarantor (even as an ideal) of her femininity. The lack of a male gaze during the girl's childhood makes her the slave of that gaze for the rest of her days. And the lack of any image reflected in the maternal mirror makes her ready to adopt whatever images are proposed to her. She will get herself up as whatever you care to name – just so long as she is allowed to go on playing the game of hide-and-seek with desire.

A woman always remembers that her earliest acting experience was on the Oedipal stage, where her role was to bring on her father, who was still standing in the wings; she never forgets the technique of coaxing men out of neutral feelings. A grim fate indeed, to be kept apart from Oedipus for years, and one with grim consequences for the woman, in her under-developed narcissism, her endless guilt-feelings in respect of a norm that lies outside herself, and the birth of her super-ego – which strikes me as being (contrary to Freud's claim) far harsher than the man's.

But a day finally dawns when signs start appearing on her body. A day dawns when she is whistled at by a boy in the street and she goes all funny inside – if not indeed funny 'all over'. She races back home: what's this? Can the long wait really be over? Is the desert going to fill up with people? And that little shadow of hers, which only yesterday could move about the place untroubled: is it now going to enter the full glare of the spotlight? This body of hers, which knew only the 'colourless', has suddenly become so brightly-coloured that the girl blushes to the roots of her hair. What else can she do? How can she move naturally from indifference to too much difference?

Two attitudes are possible at puberty. On the one hand, the girl can enjoy to the full the fact that she has finally made her way to the field of desire (at 13 or 14), and she can now do everything possible to make up for lost time, laying it on thick, showing herself off in order to draw this fabled male gaze which seems to be the answer to the eternal question: 'Am I really a woman?' If up to that point she has done everything possible to provide proof of conforming morally to the norm for little girls – being good, being quick, being nice – now she will set herself to provide evidence of conforming to the physical model of the older girl. Nothing and no-one will ever be so intolerant in matters of appearance or dress as the girl of 13 or 14! This is the point at which opposition to the mother breaks out openly, for her daughter wants to be a woman, but not, above all not like her mother! With her she has never experienced anything but different-ness, and that is not going to change now. Apparent (but actually non-existent) mother–daughter homosexuality: mother is the woman she has rejected for being the 'other woman', better endowed than herself, and the woman she will go on rejecting now, even as the similarity of their bodies becomes obvious. But now it is the daughter who is better provided: she is the one who gets the looks, and she will be all the more arrogant on the strength of that, because from now on she is 'on top'. As for the adolescent homosexuality which the mother has indulgently watched shaping up as a potential *rapprochement*, the daughter has neither room nor time for it and goes on pushing her mother aside, even when to all appearances she has just caught up with her. Caught up with her and passed her, for in adolescence the mother–daughter conflict is made to stand on its head.

'Oh, she's horrible, just horrible, if you only knew', I hear from despairing mothers. Yes, I do know. But do you know how long your existence as a woman has been a threat to her little girl's body? No, you do not. That is something mothers do not know, any more than they realize that this is the time when old scores are to be settled on a woman-to-woman basis, and that they have to put up with it. Now it is the mother who is 'left out', and her daughter makes no bones about letting her know it, even if it means calling her an old woman. After all, she's been called a little girl, a child. Those, surely, are the sort of terms that put people outside the dialectic of desire. Is it not the case that the woman's desirability is always a matter of age, and is age not the *bête noire* of all women? Women, chafing at being too young, only to panic later about growing too old.

The war which the mother has unwittingly been waging on her little daughter now turns into a war on herself waged by her adolescent daughter, for this daughter has never forgiven her mother for keeping the father away from the cradle. And it is perfectly true that the mother, by monopolizing the babies, has kept father and daughter apart. There can be no surprise if the daughter has boyfriends as her form of revenge. The daughter seems obsessed by the fact that her mother might take away her 'love-object', come between her and her love, just as she came between father and daughter long ago. As the girl moves into the Oedipal phase, she has only one fear: that her mother will once again stop her from getting through it. And that is why she fights her mother. Let every woman reader take a moment to think about this: is there not, in her love for her mother, a whiff of 'reconciliation'? Reconciliation which often goes back to her marriage or the birth of her first child; to the moment when the young woman can cease to feel threatened by the existence of her mother? For now it's her turn to be a mother.

On the other hand, the second possible outcome at puberty is the abrupt cessation, the refusal of change: the little girl, familiar with the intermediate, refuses to enter the field coloured by the signs of sexual identity and desire; and thinks long and hard about the colour 'woman'. She will typically go in for sexless clothes, and refuses anything that would make her look feminine out of horror, because for her it brings about the possibility that she might be turned into someone else's object. Sometimes she chooses to bind her breasts so as to prevent them from showing; or else she dresses in very loose clothes, so that no-one will be aware of her new woman's shape.

She has felt too much hatred for this woman to want to become one now herself, and she rules out any sign of femininity. She may even go so far as anorexia, for by refusing to eat she can, for a while, hold up the natural course of the body – stop the breasts from developing and periods from starting. In general, these girls reach a level of intellectual attainment that is disproportionately high compared with the average for their age and sex, so proving that since the redirection of libido on to the body has not taken place, they are still actively involved in sublimation.

The anorexic chooses solitude (for she feels very different from her friends and companions, all identified with the desirable girl) against desire.

What these girls are telling us, surely, is just how much is at stake in the switching of direction of libido which takes place in women when the distinctive sexual features appear. This symptom, affecting only girls, does deserve to be viewed, then, as a response to a dialectic of change: that change which has been refused because it would involve an unacceptable identification with the mother. While the boy of the same age carries on his steady development towards manhood, and has had no decisive choices to face since the end of his anal struggle with his mother (which will or will not have allowed him to accede to the rank of man by putting aside the dominance of the mother), the girl lives out, at an advanced stage in her life, a dramatic choice: 'Am I or am I not to put on the colour "woman"'?

The 'featureless desert' has turned into a world with bumps and hollows, the cynosure of all eyes. The little girl's solitude vanishes with brutal suddenness: she who, ever since she was born, has lived by dreams, has to stand and face the gaze of others, feel and survive the weight of desire.

Now she has to live her life in the present, when all she has ever known is the future.

And it will be the same process, just as brutal, not many years later, when she will be forced to speak in the past tense, once more from outside the field of desire. There too we shall find panic reactions, refusal of the situation: there will be much smoothing out of wrinkles, concealing of age, dyeing of hair. But the brutal suddenness is a feature of all these changes; a woman's life has about it none of the unbroken flow of her partner's.

A woman's life, then, is always 'too much' this or 'too little' that. There is never any stable balance between this body which attracts too much attention or not enough and this mind in search of orderliness, of a gradual and logical development. This is what makes mothers say that their daughters are more complicated than their sons. But what is more complicated is their body; and that is something that will be with them as long as they live.

To try to line up the active period of women with their genital sexual life is lunacy. Do that and you end up with a lack of continuity that must undercut any genuine achievement. If woman's actualization is a problem, it is because of repeated attempts to equate what she can produce with what she can reproduce, so that, for that very reason, women have seen their lives reduced to a few years of active reproduction measured against a great many years of boring emptiness. This body of hers that is too fertile in promises has acted as a handicap on her mind: the man has taken sublimation away from her, but seconded her to child care. In short, her body has been used to deny her mind. This is what makes women so angry now; this is why they are in no hurry to get involved in reproduction.

Continuity/discontinuity: this is the rack on which contemporary woman has been stretched. She realizes that the man, even as he sings the glories of her body, has put forward that same body as an argument for shelving her mind.

8

The spider's web

> She was going to give them so much love that their whole
> life, made up of care and loving-kindness, would lose all
> meaning away from her.
>
> Boris Vian, *L'Arrache-coeur* (Paris, 1962)

How can we describe the thing that we are not? How are we to talk about what we do not immediately experience? All that I as a woman can do is tell what I can see of the life of the little boy, and pass on what I hear about it whenever the man drops his guard.

And just what have I seen? Well, first of all, there was Thierry, who was part of the world where I grew up, and who from the time he was 2 until he was 12, would cup his hand round his precious 'thing', to protect it. Against whom, or what? Had he any idea? He had become the butt of family jokes: 'Are you scared it will fly away?' 'Maybe you think it hasn't been fixed on right?' And then there was the trick question asked one day by the uncle who knew a bit about psychology: 'Come on, now: if you're all that afraid they're going to take it away from you, who does it belong to? I thought it was yours?' And up piped Thierry, to the astonishment of everybody, including his mother: 'It's Mummy's.' In general, embarrassed at being caught revealing his unconscious fear, he would either take his hand away for a minute or two, or he would get away from the adult who was going on at him. In my photograph album there are several group photographs where you can see Thierry in the Botticelli Venus pose. For, unlike what Botticelli believed, it is not the woman who tends to hide her sex if caught naked; it is the man.

How is it that throughout Greek and Latin statuary this gesture is so often attributed to the woman? It is surely far more likely that she would hide her breasts, coveted as these are by the man.

It seems, naturally enough, that each tends to hide away whatever the other sex most envies; and for a little boy, what his mother might covet is his sex.

I also have in my possession a film in which, out of all the cousins immortalized by the camera that day, only Hervé is caught coming out of the house with his hand in his flies – his favourite gesture (was he looking for reassurance, checking that his 'thing' really was there, and that his mother hadn't yet got it away from him?).

And when Thierry and Hervé are grown up, will they even remember this familiar, unconscious, little-boy gesture of theirs? I'm prepared to bet that they will have forgotten it, but that their fear of 'woman' will have turned into something aggressive in their behaviour towards women, and that they will be spoken of as 'macho'. They will have forgotten that they spent their childhood years in a wild attempt to protect themselves against their mothers' desire, and, now that they are grown up, they will find nothing odd about the fact that certain products are marketed with them in mind: the after-shave that is called 'Sauvage', the wool that is labelled 'pure' and 'new', the underpants called simply 'Homme', the car described as 'the ultimate challenge', and so on.

You must all know plenty of Hervés and Thierrys, both young and old. Take a good look at them. Watch how they shift imperceptibly from self-protection to self-defence. The whole process happens automatically, uninterruptedly, smoothly. Starting out from fear of the mother, they end up dominating women.

And yet, when they were little, it looked as if *she* had won. When I think of the number of times, in my consulting room, I've seen them, their eyes always turned towards their mother's, not uttering a word, while she gave a detailed account of everything her child was saying and doing – or rather, not saying and not doing. Then, as soon as the mother had gone out of the room, the child would sit down again, take her place, answer my questions. And there was always one question in particular, apparently so untroubling – 'What's the matter, then?' – that could always bring tears to his eyes as he answered 'Her', or fury to his heart as he blurted out: 'It's because of her.' I don't need descriptions or explanations, I understand, I've got the message, I know the Oedipal picture so well. It is the mothers who don't know it, don't understand it. Has anyone ever talked to them about the risk that comes from their continual closeness to their child? Apparently not, since they make no attempt to hand over responsibility to anyone else.

As Freud says, mothers would be amazed if anyone told them that when they look at their children, their gaze has in it not only love but desire for the opposite sex, and therefore desire for their sons; and that no male child can take that on without feeling afraid. This, as we have seen,[1] is a fear which does not appear straightaway, since the primary symbiosis seems to work to the little boy's advantage, and even strengthens his narcissism. This fear only appears at the anal age, when the child has to take the strain of learning to be clean and of discovering the difference between the sexes.

The source of evidence for the difference between the sexes is the mother (she who is closest to the child), both for the girl, who witnesses her superiority, and for the boy, who sees her with 'something missing' where the sex organs are. If witnessing the mother's superiority sets off envy in the girl, the sight of his mother's inferiority sets off *fear* in the boy, for, as Freud says, every child believes that everyone else is made in the same image, and if his mother 'hasn't got one', it can only mean that she hasn't got one *any more*, that she's lost it, etc. This 'something missing' in the mother's body is immediately regarded as a loss, as some kind of disappearance, as a possible castration. Here we have it, then, this dreadful affliction that hangs menacingly over the rest of the boy's life: he fears castration. He is afraid that any human with 'something missing' (and therefore all women, including his own mother) will attack him, who 'has one'.

The mother, then, is a twofold danger: she 'hasn't got one', and she unconsciously wants the man's – even if the man is her own son. This the little boy experiences as *threat*: in Freud's terms, fear of castration. The whole of Freudian history is there: castration anxiety will take hold in man and drive him to defend himself, first against 'the woman', then against women. Mere male fantasy, this claim that women feel 'penis envy'. This envy is a figment of the man's imagination, hunted and haunted by the idea that she is going to take it from him: that she may actually castrate him.

If psychoanalysis had been written by a woman, no doubt there would never have been any mention of castration. Castration is a little boy's notion; envy is a little girl's.

You will have noticed that when they get to adult years, in practice the woman tries to acquire the greatest possible sexual distinctiveness, while the man tries to preserve his, as far as he can, by commanding respect as a male. Envy belongs on the woman's side of the line. There is no end to women's envies, women's dreams: it seems as if they are always waiting for something else, something different. Defences belong on the male side. Men keep accumulating powers that will consolidate their supremacy. In the end, the woman's strong desire to take, to have (a highly generalized desire, by no means only – perhaps indeed hardly at all – directed at the man's sex: is it not true that every little girl dreams of being a queen, that is, of having everything?) triggers in the man the fear of being possessed, robbed, trapped, as he so often puts it.

As 'they' so often put it, when they are on the couch:

'I feel I'm stuck to my mother. I just can't *get away from her*. I always feel she's right behind me. I ought to really shout at her, smash the place up, do something.'

'She's there, she's always there. How can I *get away from her*? Even if I do go somewhere hundreds of miles away I know she'll always know everything about me.'

'How hard it is to *get away from* one's mother!'

'Shall I ever manage to break this thing that *pins me down*, pens me in, binds me continually to her?'

'I'm always doing this with my hands – the gesture of *pushing away* something that makes me feel uncomfortable – something like "her", who was always there!'

'Yes, that's it: cut the umbilical cord. Cut it, break free of her, get away from being *caught*, etc.'

'I've got to sleep with a woman so I can say I've done it, I'm a man, I've *got the upper hand*, that's all the proof I want.'

Is it not true for all of us that the man in our lives is more or less taken up with the idea of keeping apart, getting away, putting some distance between himself and woman? Is he not striving by every possible means to differentiate himself from her in role and in character? Even if it means dressing us up in certain qualities which he deliberately forgoes: intuition, gentleness, tenderness, and so on.

He, meanwhile, puts up defences all round: he will not be gentle, or loving, or sensitive. That is where difference must be set up, so that he won't fall back into resemblance, fall back into the feminine, so he can avoid castration. The man acts out his part as man out of fear of being equated with the woman; while the woman acts out her part as woman so as not to be equated with 'nothing'. Each is locked in a dreadful stereotype, for fear they might deviate from the norms of their sex; for it seems that that sex is still not clearly enough established.

Both the closing off of the boy and the feminizing of the girl are brought about by one and the same pattern of relation: the relation with the sex of the child-rearing mother. This morning a woman said to me: 'A woman works out where she stands by reference to another woman.' Yes, but in fact both sexes work out where they stand by reference to a woman; seldom, or too late, in relation to a man, for he has no share, or virtually none, in child-rearing, both in terms of the family and in broader social terms.

But let us turn once again to the history of the boy. As we saw, his first experience of intense anxiety comes when his mother asks him for the contents of his bowel: he gets the idea that she is after 'something else'. For even if he hasn't seen with his own eyes that his mother has no penis, he has asked (as the girl did about breasts) if his mother is like him (his own first thought), and his mother has answered that she 'hasn't got one'. He has already had a fright, and worked out a whole scenario in which he too might have 'it' taken away from him. And now here is his own mother asking to be given something of his – not the happiest of moves. Asking for something from someone who is afraid of losing part of himself: hardly, you'll admit, the ideal approach. But what other way is there? The boy does, after all, have to learn to be clean.

He, in any case, has a different view, and makes the first move in the anal battle. He will do all he can to avoid giving away anything; he'll try to trick her, pretending not to need the pot when she puts him on it, then letting everything go in his nappy the next minute. Or he'll do it just before the ceremony is due. Maybe he'll be dirty all the time. So what? What is it to him? What matters is escaping unscathed from maternal desire, getting away from her and her demands. So that the boy's toilet training will drag on and on. There can be no giving in until he has found out how to score a different kind of victory over her, by becoming aggressive, moody, awkward (the baby boy may be more pliant than the baby girl, but the boy-child is more difficult than the girl-child): he puts up a constant display of opposition.

This is the start of a small-scale war. In any case, we can all see that, even in the games he invents, the boy is endlessly playing war. If he hasn't any soldiers or horses, he'll always find a way of setting up, somewhere, somehow, the play of opposing forces. For him, everything comes down to 'stronger' and 'weaker'. He sees himself as Zorro the victorious, Tarzan the all-conquering; dreams of being a pilot hurtling through space faster than anyone has ever done. The boy's fantasies always have to do with winning. This is how, by stages, the man develops a defensive–aggressive approach in everything he is and does. His very way of talking will be stamped with it: his speech will be tough, slangy, coarse, even filthy. Sometimes that hangs on in him as a myth of maleness: it's OK for a man to be 'crude'.

But for various reasons it may happen that the little boy can't make it on to the classic road to 'maleness'. He will go off in a different direction, giving up the struggle because 'the enemy' is too strong. The direction he takes is that of regression. Seeing the effort that is called for, he just gives up, he dies: becomes apathetic, goes on wetting and soiling himself, shows no interest in anything for fear he might fall back into the supposed desire of the mother or the parents. In a word, he would rather not grow up than have to face war and risk castration. If being an adult means passing through the desire of a woman, he'd rather stay a child.

And if it was just one woman, it wouldn't be so bad; but it's women. The little boy is surrounded by them! They make up virtually his whole world, and if he leaves his mother's world, it will be to go to nursery school, where he will meet the woman who runs it, then on to primary school, where his teacher will be a woman. On all sides he is surrounded by women. When his teacher is standing over him, his father seems remote indeed. It is a disaster that the early training and education of children lies almost exclusively in female hands. For the boy can find no way out of his castration anxiety, surrounded as he is by all these people who 'haven't got one'. I shall never forget, as long as I live, my son's despairing look when I lifted the hat that his teacher had deliberately pulled down over his face as a mark of shame. There and then I discovered the bottomless pit of humiliation he felt himself pushed into by this creature who 'hadn't got one'! He looked at me first of all to see if I would understand, and which way I would jump. Then, when he saw that I grasped what it meant to him, he burst into sobs and then, almost immediately, into angry shouting. Jérôme was then just 4. His unconscious was like an active volcano, while his teacher was 30 and had no idea what a little boy's unconscious is like. She thought she had simply taken a particularly mild way of punishing him for disobedience. At that precise moment I realized that if it had been a man who had meted out this punishment, Jérôme would have felt no need to hold out against it.

Nothing is harder than to hear sentence being pronounced from the other side of the divide. If the children are mixed, the teachers should be mixed as well, so that boys and girls can stand on an equal footing before those who hold power. This is something quite simply ignored, perhaps not even known in a country like France where, because no independent social role has been found for women, they are continually handed the care and education of the child.

The more the boy grows, the more organized his 'anti-woman' defence becomes, so that, by the time he reaches adolescence, he is oddly ambivalent about girls, whom he is at once eager to meet and anxious to keep at arm's length. And so, for the most part, he goes out with the girl for a while, so he can satisfy his curiosity about the opposite sex; then, very rapidly, he gives out that he has dropped her because she's a 'silly bag'. Oh wonderful insult, so right for what the boy wants to express: it is because her sex is female that she has just been rejected, not because she is silly.

In this period of adolescence, the boy is apparently no longer afraid of women. He is above them with his general contempt for womankind; he dreams of subjugating them, and then, a little later, of 'screwing' them. Is there any way in which the sexual act, on the man's side, would not contain fantasies of domination? And how could the woman possibly get what she hopes for from it, since she will lose all right to be the one who decides to do it or takes the lead in it? The man will always want to be the guarantor of the female orgasm. As a result of which we have to reach a climax the way he likes it. There is only one grid for orgasm: the one invented by men. Recent claims made by 'new women' are frightening to men, who fear that they may lose their supremacy; which is why men are so hard of hearing when the talk is of sexual pleasure in women.

It is on account of the man's need for dominance over the woman that he takes such a dim view of the new abortion law, which has restored to the woman full control of herself and her desire for a child. This man who will never know the distended belly cannot bear that someone else, a woman, should have a less than exalted valuation of it. He will not admit that this woman, whom he insists on keeping under his sway, should have views and problems of her own. This man whose own body can never carry the mark of love will not allow the woman to have any such desire, unless it is transformed into the desire to have a child; for at least in the child he could see his mark. While if she wants to have an abortion, he gets the idea that she only ever wanted sex for her own ends, so that in the very moment of pleasure, she got away from him. That is something he cannot bear, which is why he can agree to contraception, but not to abortion. He will put up moral or medical objections, but basically what gets him is that the woman doesn't see things the way he does, and that she is taking the liberty of living them differently.

When all's said, if we women keep finding along our way a man making a nuisance of himself, then it is we who have made him the way he is today. This women's cage that we're in – we put it up ourselves, not knowing we were doing so, not wanting to do so, and unable to do a thing about it. The spider's web that we have woven round the little boy is the very web in which, later, we shall be trapped. We shall never have the right to leave the area assigned to us.

The actual spider will be the man, and we are his prey as long as he lives; all because we insisted on ruling his early years, and surrounding his life as a young male with rules and regulations. No woman should be unaware of the traps of the maternal unconscious; no woman should accept to bring up her son on her own; no mother should remain neutral at the increasing hold women have on the upbringing of little boys. But were you aware of any of the things you have learned here? Who would have been willing to tell you? Psychoanalysis itself, was it not – is it not still – largely in the hands of men? Perhaps even in this there survives the male pleasure of dominance through knowledge.

There will have to be women alongside men if science is to get away from ignorance of the world; there will have to be men alongside women if growth and training are to mean having time, not doing it.

9

The impossible encounter

Yes. I want to be your wife right now so that I can be with you alone, not hearing any voice but yours.

Federico García Lorca, *Blood Wedding*, in *Collected Plays*, trans. James Graham-Luján and Richard O'Connell (London, 1976), 238

Overcoming even the man's great 'anal' fear, overcoming even the woman's great 'oral' demand, the dream of love takes hold. Now, matching each other step for step, the two of them go off in search of the lost symbiosis. With the same alacrity, they set out for the 'dangerous' encounter, with its echoes of that other meeting, many years before, with Jocasta. Loving is the conscious search for what we never had, and more often than not, the unconscious rediscovery of something we have already known.

A man comes through a cruel, pitiless war with another woman, his mother; a woman has emerged from the featureless desert of her childhood. They meet, they exchange words, they touch, they have the feeling that they already know each other, as people do who have come from the same place (which they have: for both, the earliest known landscape was the face of the mother) and by the same route (which they have not: we have seen how very different were the paths they took). But symbiosis is already at work, stronger than words. They hardly dare speak to each other in case it vanishes. Each still bears the scars of failure with Jocasta: the boy who was denied access to the body of the woman he loved, the girl who was denied the desire of the woman she loved. But now it seems as if what both had to forgo can be made good by the 'I love you' that can knit body and mind together once again.

The encounter is a unique moment in which conscious and unconscious flow into each other. The wish comes true, the dream comes down to earth to take the form of a face like no other: the 'love-object' for which both have been secretly waiting.

Ever since the mirror stage, when we came out of symbiosis with the mother and discovered what it is to be alone, each of us has been waiting for that other moment which, by putting an end to the duality first discovered then, would restore the primary unity. Love is an attempt to go back through the mirror, to put an end to differentness, to give up the merely individual; all for the sake of symbiosis. (It is surely the same fantasy which will drive us to cross the body-barrier too, and go on into sexual union, imagined as the losing of self-awareness and the regaining of the boundless 'oneness' that had been divided between two bodies.)

Love is the extreme form of the desire for a single identity for two people, the violent assertion of the primitive fantasy of oneness with the mother. Disparity, differentness, asymmetry become, as soon as love appears, matching, similarity, the perfect symmetry of two desires.

'Love is blind', as the saying has it; and very true it is, for the 'pleasure principle', always present in our lives, drives us to search for the ideal fusion with the mother: a fusion which we have left behind us and which we increasingly long to find through the loved one. This will lead us to confuse dream and reality, to a point where we take one face for another and merge one smile with another. The more we want to see the 'ideal object', the more confused our seeing becomes. We are in thrall to the mirages produced by our unconscious. So it comes about that the loved one's faults will be played down in favour of the good qualities; and if that is impossible, they will be adapted to become points of resemblance between the partners. In love, everyone is a dreamer. But is there any better way of countering the irreparable solitude learned in the mirror stage? Is there any other cure for the injuries left inside each one of us by the maternal unconscious? The couple is the fantasy of finding again, at last, a mother whom one has never yet met: for the woman, desiring; for the man, not stifling. It is the dream so well imagined by Verlaine:

Je fais souvent ce rêve étrange et pénétrant
D'une femme inconnue, et que j'aime et qui m'aime
Et qui n'est chaque fois ni tout à fait la même
Ni tout à fait une autre, et m'aime et me comprend.[1]

Once this man or this woman has been found, all concerned ought to live happily ever after. But that would be to reckon without the second unconscious principle at work in love: that of *repetition*. It drives us to re-enact whole situations, to go through, again and again, profoundly familiar patterns of feeling: this woman is indeed neither 'tout à fait la même' nor 'tout à fait une autre' – which is to say both that she is not the mother we knew, and that she is somehow connected with her.

If the fantasies born of the pleasure principle have made it easier for the encounter with the love-object to happen, the principle of repetition will tend to shift this love back towards the earliest love-choice, the mother; and the outcome will not always be a happy one. For we shall never again go back through the mirror without dragging along behind us the whole baggage of our Oedipal or pre-Oedipal history with the mother. And if, in the early days of love, everything that had once been harmful or hurtful is conjured away by the working of the pleasure principle, the only outcome is that these things reappear in the characteristics of the chosen one, who becomes, as a result of the principle of repetition, the site of infantile reminiscences more or less closely connected with the real (the phenomenon of projection), and very closely connected indeed with the earliest fantasy of all.

What makes for difficulties in a life shared by two people is the involuntary persistence of acts and feelings originally directed at 'another', which by way of the transference which occurs in love, begin to reappear within the love-relation itself. What the couple has to live through, with greater or lesser honesty, is the harsh fact that adult love comes second to the object-relation that bound us to our mother. For how can either partner find the 'mother' (we have seen that the man moves on from the mother to the woman and the girl moves on from the mother to the man, regarded as substitute-object in sexual terms) without the shadow of Jocasta falling across the scene; the trap, the prison that she was for her son, the strange insatiability that she provoked in her daughter?

The fear, for the man, that he will once again be shut in; the fear, for the woman, that once again she will not be loved or desired enough: these will be the two constants of love, and they indicate how indelible is the mark left by Jocasta at the cradle stage.

If it is to her that the powerful charms of love are due (through the desire to return to the primary symbiosis), it is no less true that the dead ends, the no through roads of a life shared by two people can be traced back to her. Let the man, anxious to keep his freedom, move away even a little and the woman dies inwardly. Let the woman, anxious to test out whether she is really loved, ask for proof and the man feels trapped again. This is the form that the dialectic of love takes, and power lies with those partners who are able to recognize the fantasies of the other but not take them for the real thing, who can go along with the game yet not be caught up in it. The man, for example, may want his woman to be submissive (so as to be reassured as to the dominance he himself ceaselessly doubts); she can put on a show of submissiveness, yet be by no means masochistic . . . . The woman may want her man to be 'devoted to her': he can grant her that without necessarily being her slave. Love is the art of compromise between the fantasy and the reality of each of the partners.

If love starts out from symbiosis, its survival requires that that stage be left behind, recognized as a 'dream'; that the woman and the man become aware that symbiosis now is as dangerous as it was when lived with the mother and that it can issue only in masochism; that is, the virtual death of one or other partner – or of both. Regressive moments can only be brief; the rest is the frequently painful recognition of the differentness that must be accepted, the distance that must be maintained. We embark on living together in order to experience symbiosis; we stay together in order to enjoy the full value of differentness. But victory over solitude can only ever be transitory, exceptional: there is no way back to the womb.

To live out fully the renunciation that this involves, to accept the full weight of this regret, to keep alive this nostalgia – these lead to poetry, to music, to painting, to anything that can still catch hold of a corner of fantasy and record it forever in the form: 'I would have wanted the world to be different, and I say this openly, not realizing that, by doing so, I am emphasizing the gap between the life I have and the life I sought . . . To the world I see, I prefer the one I carry within me, in my most secret places.' That is the artist's fantasy: he refuses the little he finds in order to live with and in the totality he imagines. In the same way, the lover reshapes the world, rethinks the 'other' in his or her own way, according to his or her own need. There is no seeing of the other as he or she is, only as he or she is needed: all this in order to heal the primary split from the mother.

The couple – the man

He has come from an unattainable idyll with one woman, his mother. What he is looking for is an idyll – attainable now – with another woman, one who is, this time, 'allowed'.

But he has not forgotten, for all that, the intense exchanges with the first woman. Was it not to her that he used to say, long ago and in all innocence: 'When I grow up I'm going to marry you'? And did he not have to back down in favour of a rival, his father? For 'she' was married to this father, even if she sometimes seemed to prefer the son. But the father was the rival who could not be dislodged, and the man goes on living in fear that his woman will be taken away from him by another man. Has 'cuckold' not always been, among men, the cruellest of gibes? Men are easily roused to jealousy. Their jealousy is not, like women's, despair at being abandoned; rather it is fury at finding themselves supplanted by someone else. In the couple, the first effect of repetition on the man is his concern to keep away potential rivals (see the ritual practices of certain African and Arab countries, all directed at proving that the woman is a virgin and therefore belongs to one man only). Because of their ancestral fear of being dispossessed of their mothers, men try to stamp their relationship to their women with the seal of their ownership; whether by way of outward and visible signs or by way of the customs and conventions surrounding fidelity. Here in France, as in other Latin countries, for example, the law deals more harshly with the 'unfaithful' wife than with the 'philandering' husband.

The second repetition, no less damaging to the couple, concerns the man's affective disposition. At the stage when his Oedipus complex was being resolved, or beginning to be resolved, he had to keep from voicing his loving feelings for his mother, and, because of that, he seems to have lost all capacity to put into words any feelings of that kind. His talk is restricted in range and affectively impoverished, for he has got into the habit of repressing affects. Many women complain that during love-making, acts too often take the place of words, which, for the woman, has the dire effect of pushing her back into the position of desirable object instead of helping her to move on into the position of desired subject.

The man is too readily silent, to the despair of a partner who so much needs the 'I love you' which can restore the unity undone in childhood. The man seems to have as little talent for healing the woman's narcissistic wound as for providing the words of love and desire of which she was so deprived in her early years. In the typical case, the man, in the wake of the traumatic Oedipal collision which is the boy's lot, has had to put behind him loving feelings, tears, other signs of emotion – all of them marks of weakness, to be associated with women. And with that he cuts off a whole dimension of love: the dimension of language. Rare indeed is the man who is a talkative lover.

When a man does show his feelings, it will be for the most part by 'having' the woman (how often does anyone say of a woman that she 'has' a man? No, of her it will be said that she gives herself, abandons herself, surrenders). Here is the effect of the third male repetition: dominating in order not to be dominated. In love-making, the man insists on being the dominant partner; in the home he is constantly on his guard against any encroachment by 'her' on his freedom (too bad if that means she has to relinquish much of hers).

From 'graceful and elegant presence', through 'home computer' right down to 'cooking machine' – any representation will do so long as it serves to keep the woman in the places from which the man is absent. For what the man is most afraid of, when all's said, is finding himself in the same place as her (as he did in the days of symbiosis with his mother). He will do anything to avoid a real meeting with the woman he has chosen to live with. And so, because of things done by the man she loves, the woman finds herself driven back on what is for her a dismally familiar pattern: providing evidence of her femininity, her domestic skills, and so on.

Femininity, then, is the prison-house in which the man makes bold to 'enclose' the woman so that he may never run the risk of finding her on the same road as himself. The man has a psychotic fear of the woman he thinks he loves. To make assurance doubly sure, to over-come his fear and guarantee his dominance, he fills their little world with his desire, he takes over the whole area of demand, from 'what's for dinner?' to 'where did you put my sweater?' (even if by chance he himself put it away). In any event, hers only to answer.

In bed, same attitudes: he makes the moves (whether they are the right ones or not). Her business is responding, and he is unlikely to give too much thought to what *she* might prefer. One has only to see how men back away from reading any article that has to do with the directions of female sexuality: that is something they prefer to take their own decisions about. We shall see later, when we come to consider sexual relations, that if she takes the liberty of naming her desire, her partner's chance of successful performance may be correspondingly reduced. There is no greater threat to a man than the express desire of the woman, which for him invariably takes on the form of an evil trap (evil because linked to the desire of the all-powerful mother).

For the most part, the man, even when he is exceptionally well disposed towards the woman he loves, will have at least ambivalent feelings about her. Moreover, in order to make sure that he is not slipping back into dependence, the man will think up a whole range of reasons for being away from home, away from the woman. In the couple, the man feels a need for freedom which is hurtfully disconcerting to his partner, who, for her part, has never thought of herself as his adversary, and whose dreams have been of oneness.

What a catalogue of miseries, and all of them stemming from the fact of repetition as enacted by the man! But what about the woman? What are the things that she keeps coming back to?

The couple – the woman

She has come from a colourless, featureless relationship with her mother and she wants the brightest-coloured kind of love. She has come from a situation of parallel lines, now she wants convergence; after the desert, she wants the oasis. She has turned away a long time since from her non-desiring mother. Her journey has taken her through solitude and sham: what she wants now from this 'other' is the words that will make all well.

The man she loves is that man who, by simultaneously valuing and desiring her as woman, can restore the inner unity so profoundly damaged in her childhood, when mother love failed to do more than set up, in her and for her, the dividedness of 'loved object' (which she was) and 'desired subject' (which she never succeeded in being).

The woman looks to love for that unity of the self which she has so far never known, since it was her lot to be first valued as a child and then desired as an adolescent. Through love she tries to reach a reunifying of 'subject who can be valued' with 'object who can be desired', so that at last she can feel herself to be a *person*. The woman eagerly grasps the chance offered her by the man so that she may be, at last, a 'satisfactory object' for someone.

It is worth noting at this point that this is the very state to which the boy, born to the Oedipal situation, acceded at once and which he is now striving to work free of; while the girl is still struggling to get there and stay there. That struggle, more or less successful, will be the great business of her life, for she too will find, lying across her route, the principle of repetition, which time after time will lead her to make the wrong choice – now too little, now too much – and so miss her chance. For the man's reunifying words, the age-old 'I love you', will not always meet her needs.

The unsatisfiedness of the early years reappears in the love-relation itself. A woman finds it very hard to go on believing that she is a 'good object', even if her partner tells her she is. She tends to retreat to comparisons with other women, now her rivals, to try to measure herself against them; which drags her into innumerable minor slaveries and duties, the need for which is obvious only to her (perfectionism applied to every aspect of ordinary living).

The repetition factor drives her to repeat continually her 'do you really love me?', but, whatever answer her lover offers, it cannot be taken in once for all, for the time is past when these words could have shaped her being. Now there is *foreclosure*: for all the strength of her desire to come alive through desiring words, she can do so only for moments at a time – to the amazement of the man. For him, alas, there is to be no end to the insatiability of his woman, who goes on endlessly asking him the same question, even in the sharings of sexual play; when, as we have seen, he would prefer these to be free of affective charge, since for him affectivity and anxiety are too often kin.

So what 'she' sees as reassurance, 'he' perceives as source of anxiety. This is the dismal result of the phenomenon of repetition for the partners in the couple. But what, if anything, can be done about it, other than wishing that what they have to repeat should not be too radically different?

For, on the strength of her demandingness, this woman will be labelled by the man as devouring. The very thing that he most feared finding on his road to manhood is right there in his bed. Hence a tendency for the man, after a time, to stop answering. For him, a flight into silence; for her, a desperate soliloquy: this is what they have been brought to by the woman's oral hunger for words.

But just as the man has always to be making sure that he still has his freedom with respect to his partner, the woman tends to explore, to test out the extent of her partner's love and, starting out from oral demands, she moves on to make all manner of demands; all intended to ensure that the symbiosis will last, that the oneness will be kept up. The man feels the trap, so long and so deeply feared, closing round him, and increases his attempts to get away from 'her', so triggering her fear and despair. She feels herself to be clutching at air, and the love-trap shuts on emptiness. For he has gone: gone for the day, gone fishing, gone shooting, gone out for a drive; he couldn't stand any more. Perhaps he has even taken himself off to another woman, a mistress who, so long as she is not connected to him publicly and socially, is no kind of trap.

This woman who has apparently sailed through a childhood free of dangerous backwaters, with all her energies concentrated in expectation of the day when there would be a life for her, now reaches the point at which she will be unable to bear disappointment. It is now that she goes through the most acute affective difficulties of her whole life. Very often she either falls back on her children (to devour them: the myth has some truth in it), or drifts into a depression, whether psychological or physical (psychosomatic disorders), which takes her eventually to doctor or psychoanalyst as the only people who will agree to take on the role of good mother that the husband has refused.

And so we can see the imbalance grow more marked as time goes by and illusions fade: each partner goes back to what he or she was; the mask of love slips off. In the life of any couple there is always a crisis point at which each becomes aware of not finding in the other what they sought. It takes such energy to fight consciously against your unconscious! Those who make the best job of it are often those who have gone through an analysis and learned to draw into consciousness as much unconscious as possible, so turning the power-relations upside down. Men and women make their entry into the world in very different ways, and this disparity takes the form, in adulthood, of a dissimilarity of desire which is hard indeed to recognize and accept.

Sexual relations as largely determined by unconscious forces

If a substantial part of the dialogue and action between the man and the woman takes place in day-to-day dealings, the other stage on which their extreme and divergent passions are acted out is surely their sexual relation. Are we not used to hearing both about 'the joy of sex' and about 'the hell of the marriage bed'? Here too there seems more often to be a convergence of different desires than any genuine similarity. Here too the pleasure principle comes in to smooth over all manner of difficulties, against the operation of the repetition principle, whose only function is to sow the seeds of panic.

Let us take the case of the man. For him, what is at issue in sexual love is the re-enactment of his earliest love relation, that with his mother; but this time with the possibility of going to bed with her, since there is no incest taboo (hence the seriousness of impotence for a man: it both prevents him from taking possession of the second woman, and signifies that he is not yet separated from the first, the forbidden mother. First stage reaction: painful, incomprehensible surprise).

If all goes well with the chosen woman, if once the need for physical possession is assuaged, the new freedom enjoyed, the man reckons that he has broken the last tie with his mother. Now that his account is squared with the woman, he feels free and ready for social involvement with other men, just as, much earlier, he had thrown in his lot with his father, after kicking free of his strong feelings for his mother. The man is therefore not inclined to spin out foreplay indefinitely: what really concerns him is the outcome, initially seen as a victory over himself. What gets in the way is the intimation that, as part of any over-all success, he has to bring about the pleasure of the 'other'. It is to get that that the man makes the greatest number of concessions (or so he thinks). So it comes about that the man who never wants to yield to any desire but his own is brought round to first-hand awareness of the desire of his partner. (We have already seen that, in what gets said on the analytic couch, the man often reveals that the ideal situation would be one, seldom found, where the woman asked for nothing and let 'everything' be done to her. No doubt for him it is: but can she force her desire into line with his, without finding that her own pleasure becomes subsumed in his? That is what keeps coming up when women talk about this among themselves.)

And this is the point at which the man who is too neurotic, too

much caught up still in unconscious dependence on the powerful
mother, is faced with the grim spectre of impotence, conjured up by
his refusal and physical incapacity to align himself with the other's
desire. Impotence, premature or retarded ejaculation – these are the
signs of the unconscious but unceasing war with the woman's desire.
The man who fails to win the battle with his woman and her orgasm
has been defeated for the second time in the struggle with the mother,
and feels useless, humiliated. What can he do to get beyond this?
What if she is refusing to accept this power of his? Far more often
than is thought, frigidity in a woman is the cause of anxiety in her
partner. What if the woman had hit on a sure way of destroying his
authority as phallocrat?

In my view, sex has no chance of recovering real status unless and
until women's struggle can be articulated, until it can get beyond the
bed. For has it not been, up till now, the only means by which they
can mark themselves off from men? It is in bed, is it not – rather
than, say, at the office or in Parliament – that men have really been
hit below the belt.

For the man, what puts the sexual act under threat is the problem
of having to take account of the demands of the woman: a process
wholly contrary to deep-seated reflex. Did he not, in order to get
away from the Oedipal mother-relation, learn to ignore 'her' desires
totally? Did the anal battle not end in a compromise: 'That's all you'll
get from me: the rest, never.'? Is the man's fear not still that 'she'
may ask for more? The bed can become the site of a power-
confrontation, and the power that men can get over 'her' may be no
more than the power she is willing to let him have.

Good sex is the middle way between self and other; for the man,
the possibility of existing without having to deny the other and her
desires. A man's potency is ultimately linked with the way in which
the little boy emerged from the anal combat with the mother. For a
man to show love, the minimum condition is that he should not equate
giving with loss.

And what about the woman? For her, physical love is closely bound
up with the way in which she came out of the unsatisfactory 'oral'
relation with the mother, and her capacity for orgasm will be
inescapably dependent on whether she finds in her partner a good or
a bad mother. A good mother, for her, would have been one who had
given her physical and moral recognition; as a result, extraordinary
as it may seem, the extent to which her partner, over the course of

the day as a whole, has thought well of her often determines whether things go well or not that night.

Again and again we come back to this question of what place she has in the discourse of the other: the Oedipal place of desire which she must not leave, on pain of banishment to the sexless body of the little girl. If the affective, caressing side of love is neglected, the woman tends to regress to a pre-Oedipal position in which her body had as yet no part in libidinal dealings with the 'other'. The little girl's body has spent so long outside the dialectic of desire that the man who is felt as most skilful tends to be the one who can, by word or gesture, make her realize that she is affectively appreciated (a reminder of the mother's love) and physically desired (something that was not forthcoming from the father).

It seems that the man's words have the power to complete the woman. For her, physical intercourse is a chance to experience herself as 'whole' in her relation with a third party; for it appears that her sexless childhood has led her into an auto-erotic position which is more fundamental than the hetero-erotic relation that is suddenly on offer. It costs a woman no small effort not to presume, or to stop presuming, that she will only ever know solitary pleasures.

If, for the man, the risk is that he will believe he is caught in the trap of the woman's demand, for the woman it is, once again, that of believing that she can only be accepted, recognized in part – just as in her childhood years. In which case, she would be entitled only to the satisfactions available in those distant days; that is to say, achieving orgasm only by herself, never with the other – the case of almost all frigid women.

I recognize that, in the male power-system in which we live, it is sometimes hard to imagine the man as anything other than the bad mother who accepts only a part of us. And sometimes a woman needs no little imagination to believe that her day-time oppressor can suddenly, when the day is over, turn into a generous mother. And yet, if she can't reach that fantasy, the overtures of her man feel like so many brutal invasions – just like those that the day has brought her. And her response to this invasion, this rape, will be the tightening of her body in vaginismus or frigidity, which are merely expressions of a refusal to let herself be penetrated by the kind of 'mother' who can bring back that earlier one who – let all women think back to her now – could crush the little girl under the weight of those sexual endowments of which the girl felt deprived.

For the woman, then, the risks of sexual failure do not depend on the same factors as for the man. They are, however, bound up with what she went through with her mother; and the man can make good what was missing from that. For a woman's sexual experience to be good, the requirement is that her partner should be (or contrive to be) seen as a 'good mother'.

Conclusions

Is love, then, an impossibility? No, for in fact the evidence shows that couples do achieve orgasm (the rate of success I leave to the reader: given the number of reports published on the subject, you will surely choose the one that fits best your own preferences).

In the moment of coitus there is a conjunction of the principles of pleasure and repetition, with the higher charge carried by the pleasure principle, which drives the individual on into the fantasy-formations that allow orgasm. The longing to be together in the moment of pleasure seems to favour the pleasure principle over the principle of repetition. 'Good' fantasies (which are not necessarily 'good', but are helpful to the individual, who can sometimes find with their help the positive side of repetition) will outrun 'bad' ones, unless the individual's neurotic disposition prevents good fantasy-activity and sends either partner back to the 'bad mother'. What is needed is for each to see the other, not as an obstacle blocking the road to orgasm (and therefore recalling the erotic relation with the mother), but as the 'through road' to pleasure (offering a way out of the relation with the mother, whether that relation was of desire forbidden or of non-desire). The mother, the earliest initiator of the child's sexuality, has left in the man the scar of desire forbidden (by the incest taboo), and in the woman, that of having no place in desire (since there is no room in the mother's desire for the little girl's erotic pleasure).

In sexual dealings between men and women, whatever survives of the maternal relation has therefore to be left behind; each has to see the other as helpful in the attaining of his or her own pleasure – something that was not the case when the child was facing the mother. The Oedipus complex is indeed as powerfully formative, as definitive as Freud had thought; but it is above all the shadow of Jocasta that continues to follow us, all the way from the cradle to the most intimate sexual play.

Any failed sexual act may be put down to vestigial infantile aggressivity which, directed at the partner, ensures that he or she is seen as the 'bad mother', the mother who will not allow the final achieving of pleasure. We need to repress firmly enough what is negative in our individual history, and to fantasize instead the positive aspect, which we must have if we are to achieve the ideal fusion of bodies, the symbiosis so deeply longed for.

Each sexual act involves us in going back through the mirror, allows us for a moment to shuffle off the mortal coil of our solitude and find the original *one*: that negation of anguish, that site of regression where we can at last be in some measure eased of our grim condition. For as human beings we are faced with the difficulty of bearing alone the burden produced by the incommunicable nature of our unconscious. Woe to the man or the woman who cannot safely regress as far as the mother; woe to the man or the woman who cannot go all the way back through the years, who has to break off at some point, for sexual pleasure will get no further. There, on the pillow, we meet once again all the complexities we knew in childhood: desire, love, hate, ambivalence. Can sexology go on keeping to narrowly behaviourist approaches when lovers, so it appears, are and have long been coming hard up against mysterious prohibitions, powers, 'internalized permissions'?

Even a couple who get on well together physically may encounter failure on any day when the confrontation, whether explicit or latent, between their rival forces has been intense. It will not be possible for either partner, that night, to imagine the other as 'good object'.

What might be helpful to the man and the woman caught up in difficulties of that kind would be for them to be able first of all to find and understand the source of the trouble, rather than just blaming the result. Helpful too would be the awareness that, in view of the human child's long dependency on adults, its prematurity at birth, the issue of power will remain fundamental in any two-person relation (the fact that at the moment the play of forces challenges only the feminine, since the responsibility for bringing up and educating small children falls to women, merely creates one more problem exacerbating the relationship between the sexes).

I actually managed to put an end to the sexual difficulties of one young couple by getting them to change their minds about who looked after the housekeeping money. Nothing more complicated than that – it just needed to be understood. I was able to free a young married man from the image of 'bad mother', which his young wife was projecting on to him, by taking up myself the place of a very harsh and unpleasant woman. One way or another, no difficulty specific to a couple can be smoothed out if the solution does not include putting an end to the projecting of the bad mother on to the partner. That is something people should know about even before marriage.

The woman ought to be forewarned of the extent of her own unsatisfiedness and its connection with the difficulty of her relationship with her mother. She should know that it is this which will drive her to make such efforts to get 'everything', and so prepare the way for the alienation of the man's desire, which is the negation of the woman's desire (the cost of which is often her frigidity).

I have met women who are 'pretend' cooks, 'pretend' socialites, 'pretend' sports enthusiasts: what will a woman not do to keep her desiring man? Has she not been trained from early on to pay the highest of prices for her desire? Women finally get to a point where they no longer know if what they reveal is what they are or what someone else wants them to be, for they have fallen back through love into conformity with the norm of the 'other'. Identification mattering more than identity – there's something that goes a long way back in a woman's life. Many of the women I see have grown unaccustomed to themselves, unaccustomed to their own desire, as the result of a marriage undertaken in the hope of symbiosis. And it is in bed that these women act out their complaints.

The man ought to be aware of his tendency to domination, and of its origin in his fear of falling back into the woman-dominated world of long ago. He has to remember that his constant tendency is to push the woman out of his path, and that for the sake of that he is prepared to use every argument, including dishonest and even downright false ones. Sometimes his great fear of the woman seems to outstrip his great love for her. Lastly he must entertain the thought that if, in order to break free of his mother, he had to constrain himself to silence and to play down his feelings, it may not be necessary to keep this 'blockade' up for ever, with this other woman who is now beside him.

Not a few people might spare themselves ugly and painful rows if they knew that they were playing parts in a well-rehearsed scene. And a little awareness of the psychological make-up of each of the partners might stop many collisions from turning into catastrophes before either party has grasped what the matter was.

They split up, with her saying 'He never really understood me', when it's her mother she's talking about; with him calling her 'a pain in the arse', something close to what he secretly called his mother when he was little. Is it not true that we are being consulted about a conflict in which the real other party is not the one we have in front of us? He thought he was 'shut in'; she thought she was 'left alone'. Were these not fantasies of their childhood? Are our clients not all talking to us about how they got on with Jocasta?

10

Words or war

> How can we speak so as to escape from their compartments, their schemas, their distinctions and oppositions . . . How can we shake off the chains of their terms, free ourselves of their categories, rid ourselves of their names? Disengage ourselves *alive* from their concepts?
>
> Luce Irigaray, *This Sex Which Is Not One* (*Ce Sexe qui n'en est pas un*), trans. Catherine Porter and Carolyn Burke (New York, 1985), 212

And then words: what are we going to do about words? Those words which so often have penned women in, which they are learning to get away from by means of other words – words which, at last, are different from those allocated to them by men.

Oh sons and daughters of the same mother, why this war of words? Why this sexism still present in language? Why this refusal to speak the same language just because one happens to be a man or a woman?

Language, born of the split with the mother, has also served to bring her back again. The object was the same; but we may ask why the way we express ourselves is so heavily marked by the sex we belong to. Why this segregation? It is brought about, surely, by patriarchal societies where men, who hold the power, also control the 'Word', and stamp it with their need for distancing from the woman, equated with the mother. It is because, for thousands of years, language has been the possession of men that it bears the trace of the anal battle with the mother and masks the fear of coming close to anything feminine, anything that has to do with the body and might recall symbiosis with *her*. Sexism in language is the doing of men who carry within them the fear of using the same words as women, of finding themselves on the same ground as mothers.

Language in our society, being masculine, is bound to have a distinctly anti-feminine aspect: this is what women are gradually discovering.[1]

In 'Latin' countries like ours, a man's first image is the image of a woman. He is bound to be taught to speak by a woman, his mother, and all his energies as a male go into establishing himself as different from her, so as to avoid 'turning into' a woman. In this early stage, the man has no way of constructing an identity other than opposition to the mother, that is, counter-identification with the woman.

Much later in his life he will establish himself by reference to his father, but, unfortunately for the rest of us, men as well as women, many men remain more deeply marked by their early relation with their mother than by their secondary relation with their father.[2] It appears that what one sex sees as a quality, the other decries as a shortcoming. This odd phenomenon is explained by the fact that the man's character, as well as his language, is built up in opposition to his mother's. In terms of identification, she remains the impossible point of reference for her son (no-one will need reminding that only the boy's language goes through an anal period of crude insults, most of them sexual and focused on the woman's body).

Since masculine language is bound to have an anti-feminine stamp, how – if they want to – are women going to speak? If they move into male discourse they must take on what is anti-feminine in it, and so talk against themselves; if they make bold to talk in some other way, they aggravate the difference between the sexes; taking a share in the very distancing process laid down as a requirement by the man himself. For it never occurs to him, even for a moment, to talk like a woman; he is a convinced believer in the existence of two natures and two kinds of speech. This is what makes me wonder if the women who clamour so loudly for their right to be different haven't fallen into the trap laid by man, whose only thought is of differentiation from women.

All the way from the 'Christiane is filling out' at age 13, to the recent 'You feminist women are digging your own grave', and finishing up, barely a month ago, with 'But perhaps for women salvation might lie in silence' – this last dropped by one of my own confraternity (or should I say 'counterfraternity' or 'pseudo-fraternity'?) of psychoanalysts: it is all, in my view, one and the same thing. The man seeks by every possible means to mark me off as 'different'. I learned something else from this particular analyst: that I, who was made to give birth, have been condemned to death (since there is talk of possible salvation for me) ever since the age of 13, perhaps even since day one. Is it not this particular differentness that the man finds unbearable in me? And so he invariably strives, does he not, to restrict me to this one function of childbearing, depriving me of all others. He has turned this advantage upside down, making it into a disadvantage: if I am programmed for that particular miracle, he will keep all the others for himself, and deny me access to them. Must I accept as segregation what I originally received as sexual definition?

How hard it is for a woman to exist anywhere else, exist in any other way than has been laid down for her by her mate! How hard she finds it to talk to him whenever she feels sure he won't like it! In any case, how could I speak a language that belonged, not to me, but to the 'other'? I might just as well keep quiet! Which is exactly what women have long been doing. Rather than get embroiled in a war, they habitually kept quiet – and men found it natural that they should. Since 'she' wanted to be the 'man's object', the woman could hardly at the same time be a subject.

The discourse of the man brings death to the woman, inasmuch as it takes away her place as subject by accepting her as object, and decides on her behalf what is good for her. Thus the woman's place and her language are defined by the man. And since the deciding was not done by her, the place that she has is that of a dead woman, and the language, that of a mute one.

So when I watch the same play being performed again and again, with the same results and the same cast; when I am simultaneously on stage and in the stalls for a show which I didn't write; when I know that the denouement necessarily involves my disappearance, I am not particularly amused – even if I know exactly how to play my part.

And so the woman finds it impossible to speak without feeling that she is bringing back from the grave a 'dead woman', all because of the transgression which she must accept and which changes her from subject into object and, immediately, inescapably, sets her over against the man's most secret desire. Can any man read what I am writing without feeling *attacked* by the very fact that I exist? I'm leaving the nursery, where he thought he had put me away for long enough. I'm leaving the dressing-room and announcing that I don't give a damn about his clothes. I'm leaving the kitchen and telling him that, if he is hungry, he can look after himself. And I end up by telling him that I was stupid to learn all these roles, just as stupid as he was not to learn them. And there's a fair chance that this will make him feel bad now, just as I feel bad that I never learned to talk, to write, to think.

That's what the birth of women means: they are beginning to exist in line with their own desire. If that falls outside the dreams or fantasies of men, it's just too bad. Couples too are finding the shared life harder and harder, all because the 'slave' has rebelled, and prefers to go without being paid by the man in 'gratitude'. Men who had thought they were safe from any further wars with Jocasta, thanks to the neat sharing out of roles, are now finding their whole system under attack from all sides. Wherever you turn, there are women letting out the 'cry' of the new-born baby – what has come to be known as the 'newly-born woman'.[3] What they are feeling, aren't they, is that for the first time they are 'doing the talking'; that at long last they are not 'being spoken'.

All these cries from all these women, all at once: what a din in the ears of men, who see no way of getting back to the peace they've enjoyed since time immemorial: the peace that belongs to the days when women were quiet, that is, dead. And sure enough, the women who have spoken up on the subject have been up till now angry, vehement, scandalized, astonished that they should have been fooled for so long (Simone de Beauvoir, Luce Irigaray, Kate Millett, Benoîte Groult, Annie Leclerc).

And then my own case. This, of course, is the area of my thinking where I feel the greatest irritation at what has happened to me because I was born a woman. For the kind of death they tried to plant in me did indeed have to do with words, with speech. If I want to speak, if I want to exist, it will be against the words of men, who have rendered me null and void. For I have never forgotten that classic male remark: 'If women do indeed know something, is what they might or might not know of any concern to psychoanalysis?'[4]

Is that not exactly where we can locate the man's panic fear of women: the possibility that she might speak up in and from the same place where he is? And God knows psychoanalysis is a particularly male place. A place where it's not uncommon to hear talk of a 'feminine' which has no connection with women. Is it possible for the language of men to be anything other than an execution, an exclusion of the woman-as-mother? Let us remind ourselves of Lacan's words: '"The woman" can only be written with "the" crossed through.'[5] A language which in fact puts a line through woman, denies her, removes her as female referent; a language which moves ever farther from anything that might recall the mother. Lacanian language is the very model of male language: a place for getting away from the woman, who brings to mind that other woman. No room in it for any except those who have left their hearts behind them and destroyed all trace of their feelings for their mother. Lacanian language is, typically, an anti-feminine discourse (even if a few women have the nerve to take up the challenge by speaking it) because its goal, as well as its effect, is to get away from the body and from affects, even if only by being esoteric in form.

Against this, what can the 'new women' say if not that, for them, language includes the body, preserves the affects and yet does not neglect concepts; totally refusing any dichotomy between word and concept? Women say that the body/mind split within discourse is the man's doing, unable as he is to get away from the idea of running from anything that looks as if it might be part of a world he has experienced as female.

Feminist women serve notice that castration has nothing to do with them. And that they are out to talk as and when they like about anything and everything! They are going to bring taboo subjects back in, to speak the forbidden words. Women are busy getting rid of the prohibitions that bore on them, for they are coming to see that it was men who had put up all these bars in order the better to shut away 'the witch'.

As women gradually cease to take the law of the 'other' as their standard, they are coming through hysteria, coming out of alienation. The feminine in language is no longer a matter of form: it is beginning to exist as content. Hitherto, a woman has been a woman by virtue of her exterior, her appearance, her speech, which has had to take a certain form and restrict itself to certain subjects.

Feminists reject the idea of defining themselves by their exterior. They are therefore abandoning the 'hysterical' as a mode. This is something that must be understood in connection with the new language of women: it is spoken from inside, not any more from outside; and it is for that reason that it affects our hearts, the very core of us. Women's new form of expression has something fascinating, something dizzying about it; its associations are with freedom, taking off, heading for measureless horizons. First there was the hyper-castration of the word; now there is its anti-castration. Women feel the need to escape in the first instance. Later they will seek their own limits – and these will no longer be the ones laid down by men.

I myself, for example, get a lot of pleasure from confronting men with their womb envy, their *Uterusneid*, after all the play they have made with my *Penisneid*.[6] I enjoy speaking out and saying what I think of them, whereas up till now I used rather to listen to what they said about me. They always talked of our frigidity – it was virtually part of the syllabus – but I am discovering their obsessive fear of impotence, the ineradicable mark of their fear of the mother–woman. Why should I not say so? For the memory of Jocasta lives on in men as well as in women; and when it comes to facing the desire of the other, we are neither of us up to much.

But the great difference between my language and that of a man is that mine is made to be grasped, used to forge a link with 'the other', whereas his has always driven me away, kept me off. And I hate distances . . . And when I am asked if there isn't a male psychoanalyst who has attempted to bring the unconscious problems of the couple within the understanding of trainees, I always feel like laughing, because I think that men are only at ease when there's a distance, particularly with women. Any move on my part towards closing that gap is felt as usurping; any attempt on my part to claim an existence is seen as castrating, by him and of him.

And of course the existence of the one does threaten that of the other. As Sartre said: 'Hell is other people.' Yes indeed, hell and heaven are what we are for each other. The trouble is that men (the poets excepted) see women as hell more often than as heaven. Is it not true that the famous 'Oh I just adore women' is nothing but the loud claiming of an adoring stance which might otherwise have gone unnoticed?

When a woman, any woman, is not heaven for her man (that is, appears frigid), has she not made a start at getting out of the hell where he had kept her? Is she not making a stand for her own share of freedom – and putting her stand before his 'stand'? There is indeed a relationship between existing and having sexual pleasure, and if men really do want us to be 'into sex', they will have to put up with us being 'into living'. It is no accident that it is since they've been speaking out, acquiring a certain power, that women have started to think about their own sexual pleasure.

They are noticing that if they accept the alienation brought by a particular social and familial role, they have also alienated their original sexuality and made it into the one the man expects.

Trying to make good the lack of male 'recognition' in early childhood, women in adult years rush towards the mirror held in front of them by men. But in this mirror the woman does not see her own image; she sees the image the man has of her. Jocasta has left her ineradicable mark on the man's heart; for this mirror holds only the image of a 'dead' woman.

Ask an alienated question and you get an alienated answer. Which is farther off course: the woman who asks the question, or the man who gives the answer? In any event, both are speaking from their misadventures with Jocasta. Because of his personal history, there is no reflection that the man can give back to us that will not be death-bringing. If we accept the share of language that he has in mind for us, we accept silence (as a male analyst so shrewdly told me). To become what the other wants us to be, to give expression to what he thinks: could any death be worse? Man is not equipped to give birth, even if woman runs to him in the hope of being 'delivered'. The only woman he can give birth to will be still-born.

'I've always been walking away from myself', a woman told me the other day. And that is just what women do: if they look in the mirror the man is holding, the only direction they can take is that of the anti-feminine. Our 'dear liar'[7] is well aware of it, but she prefers lying to 'dying'. Once again the woman must make the sacrificial offering to Jocasta. She who was out looking for life has plucked death. Remember Annie Leclerc on men: 'The only thing you've ever really gone on asking us to do is to keep quiet. And in strict truth, no greater demand could be made. Beyond that you would have to demand our death.'[8]

If we come into being by way of the words of a man, we lose the chance of attaining what might have been our existence, and are plunged for ever into his, which goes by way of our disappearance. There's always Montherlant, that notorious anti-feminist, to give us the woman as a moth drawn irreversibly closer to the man's flame until she burns her wings. Does he not put these words in the mouth of Inès in *La Reine morte*: 'The day I came to know him was like the day I was born.'? Does he not make Ferrante the king comment:

'I have observed that every woman circles obstinately round what will surely burn her.'?[9]

What is at issue here is the woman's wish to be born, to come into being, which runs up against the man's wish for her death. And Inès will find death at the hands of the man from whom she sought existence.

Is it not invariably the case that women seek existence from men who can only refuse to let them have it? Here he is, this man for whom she has waited so long, this man whom she has idealized so much – and what happens when she meets him? She finds out that, as a man, he cannot give her what she seeks.

Surely it is madness for us to try to get from him what we didn't get from the woman–mother. Where would the man go to give an answer to this woman who sees in him the guarantor of her moral and physical being? Inside the 'fortress' which he has learned to erect between himself and women. He has decided that he will make no more allowances to this creature who took far too much from him when he was little and unable to defend himself. Now here she is, offering herself up as a prisoner. Well, just let her find out how awful it is to come into the world at the hands of the other sex. Wants to have her turn at Oedipal feelings, does she? Well, so she shall, and beyond anything she could have asked for. And from that Oedipal sequence it will be no easy task for the woman to break free. So she wants to 'get herself fancied'? She'll be fancied all right, but the price will be grim enslavement. She will get all the things the little boy went through long ago. She will be desired, but tied down. She will give in to blackmail, on pain of being rejected. In short, the woman will, in her relationship with the man, run into everything that the little boy suffered in his relationship with mother.

Oh he loves her, all right – but he is the one who sets the terms. He accepts her, all right – but only if she 'obeys' him. He protects her, all right, but only if she 'gives up her freedom'. And then finally he is unfaithful to her – after all, that's what his mother did with his father. The man is engaged in settling scores, but it is the woman's Oedipal development that will pay for that. The Oedipal relation she had so longed for as a girl will be all she knows, as soon as she is someone's wife. But what an Oedipal relation it will be! What a father to have it with! For the man has forgotten the most elementary rules of language, forgotten how to conjugate the verbs, to string together the few words needed to make a loving sentence. Often enough, baffled at what is being asked of him by this woman he loves (thinks he loves), he says: 'But what do you want me to say?' He really does not know what to say to this woman. For what he has learned is, essentially, how to fend women off.

And in any case, he would surely find it far easier to say nasty things to her than nice ones. That is what many men disclose during analysis; for example: 'She wants me to tell her I love her, but I can't, because I have to keep her at a distance.'

How could anyone hold it against them? How could anyone reproach them for not wanting to make any more presents to Jocasta? They can no longer give pleasure to a woman without remembering the intense pleasure their mothers got out of them.

In the name of the mother, then, the daughter-in-law will be denied words. Anyhow, everyone knows that men are no better at talking to the one than to the other, and no good at all at intervening whenever there is conflict between mother-in-law and daughter-in-law. They just say nothing, since they can find no words to convey a choice which is never particularly clear: he, the son, 'object' for the 'mother', who is defending herself against his 'woman'. Even as he strives to get away from the woman he sees day in, day out, he is still stuck with the score he has to settle with the woman he no longer sees. Caught between their mothers and their wives, men, you might say, no longer know *which* way to turn.

The social inequalities that women labour under are kept going by men, in the name of their still unavenged childhood: because they were once the locus of pleasure for their mothers, women will be no more than 'disposable goods' for them.[10]

But for some time now, oddly enough, women have left off besieging the male fortress, and taken to asking questions among themselves, talking among themselves, as if they had at last realized that answers from men could only be misleading or worse. They are answering each other, they are getting past the dangerous female rivalry engineered by men, they are at last discovering the resemblance – so eagerly sought and yet, from childhood on, never there.

The adult woman is the true mirror for any other woman: sending back the image, not of witch, or tart, or man-eater, but of a woman like herself. The homosexuality that could not work at the outset, because of the bodily disparities of mother and daughter, is now available. But after how long? How many wrong turnings and how many miseries – not the least of which, for the little girl, was fantasizing the man as good mother, when the 'Oedipal' man she actually met was her worst enemy – did it take to reach this point?

For centuries the basis of the identity of men has been that of counter-identification with the woman, reduced to a maternal stereotype and, because of that, kept within clearly defined social areas and forms of language. It appears that identity in women is being built up from the realization of a shared slavery, a shared silence about men. What was silence-as-acquiescence is turning into speech-as-opposition. Men are amazed: and yet they are not unfamiliar with language as opposition to the power of the 'other'. Indeed, where women are concerned, it's about the only kind they are familiar with.

This homosexuality of speaking style, so necessary to the identity of women, is something they are finding very hard to get going and keep going, for men, by continually referring to 'good looks', have so set women against one another that each woman has become a dangerous rival for the other. Feminists have fully grasped this, as can be seen from their pressing first of all for an end to the ugly farce called 'being attractive', so that a new kind of relationship between women can be brought in – one from which hating and comparing have been banished – so that the world can see and hear a genuine woman's language, not just women going on about things like men.

Are we saying that a woman, if she is to 'born into the world', needs another woman who is not her mother? That a woman can have no narcissistic mirror except a body like her own? But is that not the same dialectic that the girl experienced in adolescence when she saw her body becoming like her mother's? Yes; but already the war between them was on. Homosexuality between them had long since been denied. It's true, isn't it, that women in feminist movements are doing no more than giving recognition to one another, by-passing the 'alienating third party' that is man, the son of Jocasta.

At last we are moving towards this new language which, maybe, will be nothing like the one that men worked out for us as feminine. Maybe we'll stop talking about recipes, clothes, babies. Who knows? We shall need time to shake free of what has been so carefully inculcated in us over hundreds of years. We shall need time to chart our course, for up till now that course has lain through reproduction. What shall we produce, when we have taken the message that production and reproduction are two different things? When our language is no longer identified with our sex, how shall we talk?

All because of our sex we had topics and modes of expression allocated to us. One has only to open newspaper or magazine to see that the great change is a long way off yet, and that the stereotypes of the 'strong' man and the woman with her 'attractiveness' are still with us. Our language has become sexist (perfumes for women, perfumes for men; watches for women, watches for men, etc.). Who will be brave enough to make a move against the bastion of consumerism, in which, as we all know, those most actively involved are women in pursuit of their 'womanly image'?

None of this can happen in a day. Men are trying to gain time, for what they are afraid of in all this is that women will no longer offer back to them that part of themselves which they have made over to women and themselves given up. They are afraid that they may have to live without the play of feeling, without words of love, since they have forgotten them all. They are afraid of ending up in an exclusively male world, since their own femininity, their own sensitivity, their own wish to please have all been left behind. If we rethink our identity, he will have to rethink his. That is the side of feminism that gets him. For the moment, he hasn't got beyond making gibes. But he is well aware that that is no way to halt so vast a movement, and that he will have to make an inventory of all that he has lost along the way since his involvement with Jocasta. 'For he has become a man, that is, a caricature of what he was.'[11]

For indeed, where our language has managed to keep the colour and freshness of pre-Oedipal childhood, the man's has been put under the guillotine of the Oedipal interdict, which took from it all affective colouring, since in the end love for the mother, so strongly marked in boys, is signposted 'Road Closed'. The male child sees himself forced to get out of the maternal kingdom, not only through displays of aggressiveness, but by language-weapons: coldness, logic, silence, absence of feelings; for these, in accordance with Oedipal law, are the marks of male language.

Men make it their business to be as cold as they like us to be warm. How are we to understand this division of affect according to sex? What is this sex which invades us, body and soul? Surely the sexual differences between our bodies are important enough for us, without having to add on differences between our minds. And if the two sex organs try to come together in the sexual act, do the two heads have to see themselves as more and more widely separated? Just because we made some attempt to recover the wholeness, the oneness of the original sex (Plato), we surely don't have to experience now the dividedness of the mind, split up into male and female entities? We were each given only half the sexual organs, but if we are only to have half a language as well . . .

This apportioning according to sex of values, roles, language itself, merely exacerbates the difference, which, instead of acting as what links us, most often functions as a bogey. We no longer even understand each other's words. How often we have heard this kind of insult directed at a man: 'Surely you must realize that that is women's talk?'; and, at a woman: 'Isn't that a rather mannish way of putting it?' If it had been possible for us, when we were little, to talk with our fathers as much as with our mothers, female language and female emotions would never have been the only set of referents that must always be either copied or avoided; and perhaps there would not now be a war of words, a war about words.

What drove the boy into an affectless language and kept him there was his need to get away from his mother. If for him Oedipal experience didn't involve her negation, language would have no cause to be sexist.

We have to move on to a point where men no longer get back at their mothers through us, where as women we no longer bring our sex into places where it has no business to be. All of us, men and women alike, are the losers, even as we think we are winning. Words themselves are treacherous, and, whether we like it or not, supply ammunition for a war that began right back in the cradle. But men have no more responsibility for their Oedipal history than we have for our pre-Oedipal drama: both are products of a patriarchal society in which the sovereignty of the mother during childhood sets off, in men, hatred of everything female, and, in women, respect for everything male. Oedipus can be allowed the right to say:

I suffered those deeds more than I acted them.[12]

And Jocasta the right to ask herself:

Love, only love. Love him who brings death? He gives you nothing, this man who takes your all; he took my all; gave me all; took back all.[13]

Are we not seeing, hundreds of years late, the beginnings of a shared understanding of what falls to our lot as a result of simply being born a man or a woman? And perhaps we are on the way to being able, at last together, to tell each other our stories, our histories; so strangely intertwined, so differently alienated.

For in their relationship with language, girls and boys do not follow the same path with respect to the same object, the mother. The girl first loses her way in childhood when, because she feels sexless, she starts behaving and talking like mother: she will be said to talk 'just like a little woman' or 'like a book'. Either way, with language she can step over, or pretend to step over, the huge gap between her and the woman she cannot yet feel herself to be. Her language, like the rest of her at this period, gives in to the law of the seductive, for that has been pronounced 'feminine': girls don't use rude words, they are gentle, sweet, not quick-tempered like boys.[14] Already she is learning what it takes to please, instead of showing what she is actually like. How many times was I to hear, because I was a girl: 'Oh Christiane, what ugly words in such a nice little mouth!' No doubt I had momentarily forgotten the difference between my existence and my appearance.

Later on, when she reaches puberty, the girl will be misled a second time; by men this time, who will make very clear to her the feminine subjects she must go in for if she wants to be attractive to them. Subjects like love, her body, beauty – anything connected with desire. The body then becomes, and remains, the subject most often talked of by women: the body whose beauty attracts, whose infirmities disturb, it is all one. In a male economy, the body is, for women, *the* subject.

So if ever they have to stand up and speak, women are afraid both of not using the 'proper words' (those laid down as feminine) and of getting away from the 'right subjects'. More often than not they will say that they haven't got the right words to express themselves (for the words are not theirs, merely those imposed on them as women); they are afraid that if they don't take up the words of their own sex they will seem unfeminine; afraid that they will be unattractive. Body/words/sex – all is confusion in the woman's own head, much as, when she was little, other people pushed confusion at her. And she shows no sign of being able to get out of the tangle. Women, it will be said, talk with their bodies; or don't talk, because of their bodies: 'As soon as I'm standing in front of a man, I go stupid, all my ideas go. I can't even respond appropriately. I feel ashamed at my stupidity, my brain stops working, I'm just a body.' This is what a woman said to me recently. The body as dam, the body as prisonhouse of the mind; the body as object of physical desire which makes it impossible for the woman to take up her place as 'subject'.

In his relationship with language, the boy must too go by way of the mother, but, here once more, differently. In order to get beyond the Oedipal position, beyond desiring the mother, he is driven to rejecting both anything to do with his body, which was an area of attraction for the mother, and anything that might indicate the affectivity with which she has too closely surrounded him, smothered him. In one single operation, the boy will banish certain subjects and take up an affectless language.

Here then is man, putting himself at a stroke beyond any connection with the body or with affective words; with 'virtually nothing to say'. The language that is, or is called male is a breaking-off language, a closing-out language (closing out the mother and her emotions). He rejects tears, emotional turmoil. He too is shut away, but in his case it is in rigidity towards his mother, in contrast to the tenderness that existed between them earlier on.

Men find it relatively easy to speak in public, to write. In any case they run no risks, since never again will they talk about themselves, but always and only about things outside them. Can what they say touch us? Seldom, since they never address themselves to the feeling part of us, but to the logical.

A man made the following startling remark to me: 'I feel I'm split in two. On the one hand, there's my body, which doesn't belong to me any more (I gave it away to them – my mother, my wife). Then there's my mind: that's working nineteen to the dozen, all the time, just for me.'

What could be plainer: a moment ago there was a woman telling me about her body that was too much present, and her mind that was absent (the omnipresent body which blocks access to sublimation); now a man is telling me about his absent body and his mind which is only working for him (sublimation taking up the entire libidinal field and leaving no room for the body). Inverse development of man and woman with respect to the same mother, leaving them both with the impression that they are poles apart. How many things there are that go on, and do not go on, in this body, this mind, all because of a woman.

But who will rid us of this troublesome Jocasta? Or, at any rate, limit the harm she does? Who if not her husband Laius, the vanishing father? He will have to be revived, brought back to his palace, where his children are. The place of the father? Wherever the child is: in nursery, bathroom, kitchen, kindergarten, at play. Wherever women hold sway, men must be there beside them, on equal terms with them, if we are ever to see children whose sexual orientation does not necessarily involve being for or against women.

What feminists now are speaking out against is a language in which woman acts as a negative referent for the man when he speaks – even when he is actually addressing 'her'. Men do this unconsciously, without even noticing; and women have decided to make them aware of this word-struggle. And I for my part have come to see my role as showing how men, if they have been brought up by a woman, can only have a language directed either defensively or aggressively at 'her' and, beyond her, at 'them'.

Surely it is the analyst who is in the best position to know that all that is at issue is a 'history', a story that can be erased and overlaid by another story – especially the one that unfolds in our consulting rooms.

Do we not see, in analysis, the man gradually recovering the affective bit of himself, so long abandoned? Do we not see his rigidity giving way to a new flexibility not necessarily involving opposition to women?

Are we not witnessing the birth of a woman who is 'other'? One who, no longer feeling crushed by the mother's superiority or bound by the man's desire, is beginning to exist in her own right, not falling back on the demand for an identity which she no longer needs, since there is no-one to deny it to her.

Rather than having to analyse, one by one, survivors of the Oedipal relation, you find yourself wondering if the Oedipal relation itself might not be managed differently, so that it didn't lead always and only into the sex war and the word war.

11

Travelling light

But his wife looked back from behind him, and she became a pillar of salt.

Genesis, 20, v. 26

Thus woman is allowed to go back to the origin, as long as it is not her own.

Luce Irigaray, Speculum of the Other Woman
(Speculum, de l'autre femme), trans. Gillian C. Gill
(New York, 1985), 151

Not the origin: she doesn't go back there. A boy's journey is the return to the native land (the Heimweh Freud speaks of . . .). A girl's journey is farther – to the unknown, to invent.

Hélène Cixous, The Newly Born Woman (La Jeune née),
trans. Betsy Wing (Manchester, 1986), 68

Must get back to me, talk about my expectations, my disappointments, my desires. Tonight is for confronting my life as a woman. I shall be talking about myself. But how? Have I been doing anything else, ever since the start of this journey? Well yes, I have, for more often than not I've been talking about 'him' and 'me' moving forward together more or less harmoniously. I've been describing our two zigzagging styles of walking, which have alternately driven us apart and, the next moment, brought us closer again. Me demanding, him refusing: these have formed the Oedipal crossroads along our two routes. At each one we took stock of how far we had to go before we could forget Jocasta.

I learned to disguise my demandingness; he learned to soften the edges of his refusals. I no longer acted on the wish that he should like me 'all round', and he didn't tell me that my mind meant nothing to him; but he went out of his way to make sure that it was used for highly specific tasks, domestic ones in particular, for which it was his proud boast that he had no gifts. In a nice way, he was offering me a folding stool that I could put beside his seat in the stalls. And the whole thing was set up so unaggressively, and he had such wide social acceptance that it was hard to fight it off. For instance, there was no question of my leaving my position as the person responsible for bringing up the children. If I didn't do it, who would?

He pretended not to notice that the burden of the children's future might well weigh too heavily in the balance of my own life.

From the moment I was married I found myself being offered a life by proxy: my pleasure was to come from the joys of others. I had to make sure that they were well, slept well, ate well, and to rejoice that everything was going well. 'My' life was to be 'their' lives.

That is what being a woman means: making do with the crumbs from the rich man's table, being grateful for scraps of a conversation which others have the leisure to pursue, getting up while the others sit where they are. It means always living one step behind what is going on and reaching the point where that is felt as a frustration which, somehow or other, allows you to blossom.

A woman is a snail whose shell everyone wants to borrow so they can keep warm, while often enough she herself is freezing. A woman is a traveller with no luggage, who turns into a porter for other people's. As for the journey, it never brings her back into her home territory, always into that of others.

A woman is someone who cannot find herself, for all her time goes into moving away from herself towards others: she is the incredible earth mother whose place is conferred on her by others, and who thanks heaven that at last she has a place – she who has never had one before.

What has been drummed into her is that her identity is something buried, not in the depths of her own being, but in the depths of the 'other''s. Always out of step with herself, always a step ahead of herself; that is what living feels like to a woman. For years she has hoped that one day her reality would fit the man's dream and that she would be able to give up pretending, lying. But no. When it comes to woman, the man's dream is unilateral and unambiguous: 'Man seeks woman friend, 20–40, sweet-natured, devoted, loving, quiet, if possible good-looking.' That's the way he likes us and that's how we behave. But it's not how we are!

But what about men, you may say: are they not similarly reduced to the stereotype of the macho? Have they any choice but to appear competent, adaptive, strong, brave, and so on? No doubt; but after a man has acted these parts all day, he allows himself – and is allowed – a hero's welcome. He comes back home and there finds all the landmarks that he knew as a child. Casually, he asks what is for dinner. He looks around for signs that he has been expected, and he finds them. His bed has been made (no knowing, no question of knowing by whom), his underclothes have been washed, even his place at table has been set. He is able to believe that he is back with his mother. He can risk a backward look: yes, everything that made up the landscape of childhood is there; he is expected.

And what about poor old me all this time? Who is there to fuss over my homecoming, my comfort, my underwear, my place at table? No-one, unless I do it. If it's mothering I want, I must do it myself. What an unbelievable piece of deception it is, where the man, taking me in his big arms, has allowed me to think that there I could at last be little and have a mother who loved and wanted me. But he is the one who does the regressing, not me; and he is also the one who forges ahead while I mark time, for there is nowhere for me to run and hide – not even here in my own home, since there is no-one to act as mother. I am the only person living under this roof who has no mother. Just as, when I was little, I was the only one who had no adequate sexual object. The story goes on: I never have a place of my own. That is always something that I must work for, fight for. And when it does come, it will be hedged about with 'ifs'. I must always be running ahead: I have to show that I am the good mother, the good cook, the good wife – on penalty of being thought to be *nothing*. It is the perfect continuation of my childhood, when I had to show that I was a good little girl so as to avoid the risk of not being a girl at all. In vain I try to cling to an image which is not mine because it doesn't come from inside me. In actual fact, I am just like everybody else – I don't want to be the mother but to have a mother. And I can find no-one willing to be that for me.

Women have to concern themselves with other people and what is yet to come for these others, but who is concerned about the fact that their own yet-to-come never comes? Must women make do with the yet-to-come of their family? And in any case, what do words like 'their family', 'my family' actually mean? Out of husband and children, how many belong to me? None. All they belong to is life: each one of them is deep in an eighty-year-long adventure, trying to get by as well as possible in this problematic world where ultimate goals are only intermittently to be glimpsed.

But it seems as if my ultimate goal is clear enough in their view: I belong to 'them'. I am 'mother', and that ought to keep me from raising all the other metaphysical problems.

Unlike all the rest of the family, I have no times when I have the right to act the child, for, if I did, who would be mother? This is the role that can never be exchanged. This is the thing you are really stuck with, for no-one ever wants to take it over from you. Women feed other people, but who feeds them? Nobody. They have to feed themselves, to function autarchically within a family where everyone else is entitled to a system of give and take. And there are days when that feels so unfair, so wrong that all they want is to throw all the shopping bags out of the window, trample on all the lettuce, smash all the eggs, and burst out crying, crying. Crying like the little girls they feel they've never been able to be, crying like abandoned creatures, crying like children, like orphans.

Of course in theory we are allowed all the signs of childhood: we are allowed to cry, to be frail, weak, incapable of extended thought. But in actual fact we are denied the right to genuine helplessness, to proper rest, to the kind of actual letting go that men demand when they get home in the evenings. Always tired, always up and doing: that is what gets us accepted by a society which is so well designed for the man's sequence of work followed by rest, and the woman's sequence of non-work followed by non-rest. The result is that women do not work on the same social tasks as men, but are distinguished by being on duty twenty-four hours a day.

What is always out of the question for women is finding some person to take over, some place to get away to, some time when they can have a rest. Not infrequently there is only the doctor or the analyst to suggest a break.

And God knows they're well aware of it, all these women who crowd into doctors' surgeries, ready to reel off the long list of their physical ailments, which are merely a pale reflection of their psychic emptiness. But can the doctor really arrange a 'break' for someone who has no clearly defined work? What is tiring is her living, living out of her skin. How can she be brought back to herself? She ran away a long time ago, back in childhood, but all that is now part of the family portrait. What response can there be to this woman who is tired of everything and everyone?

What would be needed is for the man who is her companion to learn to offer her the possibility of dropping out occasionally; to take his turn at being the provider, night nurse, sick nurse, so that she can, so that at last she can fall back on someone, instead of having to fall back on the doctor.

Men will have to give up their peace and quiet so that women can find theirs. Men will have to abandon their Oedipal patterns occasionally so that women can discover theirs. Husbands will have to stop acting the child so that wives can stop being the mother.

Until now men have had a ready answer: 'We haven't the time, and our wives have'; but women, by going to work, are making a different rejoinder, for they no longer have the time to be exploited in family terms and enslaved in conjugal terms – they have no more time than men have. So now there will have to be some plain speaking about the right to regress; it's going to have to be shared out, not, as before, by sex, but as a function of the needs of each member of the couple.

The new problem posed by women working concerns their right to regression and their access to sublimation.

Sublimation: the missing sector in the lives of women-and-mothers. Once regression had been lost to them, they found themselves (as Freud said) without sublimation. For sublimation is the act of deploying one's primary drives 'elsewhere and otherwise'; for example, instead of eating, one may give sustenance to the mind by some well-chosen reading. Like the man who, having had a meal, goes on to read his newspaper. His wife, meanwhile, goes on busying herself in the kitchen, for, beyond the meal, there is the after-meal: clearing up, washing up, putting away, and so on. How could she find a way of deploying her drives 'elsewhere and otherwise', since when she has got everything done, she will be tired and have no libido left over to expend in different form? For a woman, the whole pattern of energy expenditure is organized in the direction of the concrete, so that she has no room to spare for the abstract. It is easy – but cheap – to say that women have no access to sublimation, when they are not given the time to go in for it. Witness this very book, which I have had so much trouble fitting into my life as working woman and mother.

If it has taken me two years to write, that is not on account of difficulties in working out what to say, but from the impossibility of finding the time to get it down on the page. I have carried this book about inside me, like a child which society was trying to stop me from producing, unlike my other, flesh-and-blood children, for whom I was provided with time, rest, certain material facilities.

One day, at a psychoanalytic congress, I could hear the distinguished gentlemen talking (nonsense) about the mother, whose phallus could only, in their view, be the child; and I found myself saying inwardly that what they were doing – oh, ever so innocently – was assigning women to that place so as not to have to meet them anywhere else, and especially not in the ground of sublimation. Since I stood up and said as much, I was treated, as we came out, to a kindly aside from the chairman of that particular session. His exact words were: 'You know, we do realize that we are unfair to you women, but we dislike being reminded of the fact.'

A sudden surge of honesty from an old hand who had noticed the dangerous downward path that starts with 'penis envy', goes on to 'penis/child' and becomes 'sublimation envy'?

'They' don't want me to think or sublimate: that's their field. Mine is the glorious role of mother; my lot, the daily treadmill of the woman who looks after others. And of course then they will look after me, make no mistake about it; they will even define me in ways that lie altogether outside what I think, far from anything I know. What they know, what they want, as they have abundantly shown, is to keep us in their service, by getting us to believe that they are 'grinding away' for us. How often have we not had to hear that famous claim: 'Let's have no complaints from you: you've got the star part.' But how often have they shown any wish to have that part? That part in the play about the woman whom nobody will mother?

They really don't know women; or rather they make no effort to know us. Concerned only with their own well-being, they have tried to sink us in their desire, and forgotten to take into account our desires, particularly our 'regressions' and 'sublimations'. Remember-ing their mother, who was always on duty as far as they were concerned, they have equated us with that mother. They have run together irreversibly the two entities 'mother' and 'wife'; and, since we are their wives, we must act as their mothers. Because mother was big when they were little, we have to go on being 'big' so that, when they come home, they can go back to being 'little'. But who is going to be 'big' for us, so that we may safely regress from time to time? For the desire to go back in time, to get back to childhood, is in everybody, men and women alike. If is unfair to divide it up by sex. From the wedding day on, men seem to have the whole house to regress in; women, only bed. But, there too, problems: the man demanding climax from his wife as something he is entitled to. Conflict in bed, conflict with this man who has felt like a bad mother during the day, and wants to turn into a good mother at night. A position often rejected by women, who reckon they have done quite enough for them for the day, thank you very much, and who deny them by forgoing their own climax. There are women whose only experience of orgasm is with themselves, because in all the rest of their lives their only experience of being mothered is with themselves.

In most women's daily lives there are no possible places or times for regression; their husbands, who had once been thoughtful and sensitive lovers who took thought for the pleasures of their loved ones, have now become equated with the two or three children greedily claiming their share of daily attention. The men believe that if she can manage it for three, she can manage it for four. In itself this reasoning seems fair enough; but for the unconscious, it is false. The man sitting over there was chosen, not as child but as affective partner; and therefore as mother. What is he doing about that? What does he know about it?

With marriage, regression shifts from one camp to the other. Women have no recourse but to mother each other (if their homosexual capacities allow that), or to regress in natural surroundings, places not taken over or monitored by men. In the name of their children, woman allows herself, and is allowed, the right to lie about in the sun on the beach; something unthinkable on her own account. She lies there, unmoving, warmed by the sun (the sun at least will not stint its warmth). Of the order of regression nothing else is left for this woman whom nobody feeds, nobody warms, nobody waits eagerly for. In that position she can get back to something like her origins: the regular sound of the waves in her ears recalling the sound of the heart when she was a foetus. For, ever since then, what a scramble it has all been, and always in the name of some other or others! Even here, what is this woman actually doing? She is supposed to be getting a tan, making herself still more desirable to the man. Is it not true that most female regressions are hidden behind the banner of 'attracting' raised by men?

The husbands go on to find all this irresponsible, disloyal on the part of their wives. But is there really only one way for a woman to get through to regression – taking something she needs and saying that she is only doing it for others?

I understand feminine shortcomings. I find them charming, and see nothing wrong in them except the guilt that goes with them. They start out from the mirror (narcissistic response needed by the woman ever since the absence of any paternal gaze), go on to little extravagances (presents the woman gives herself since no-one else gives her any), and so often end up in overeating (of the good things which the partner often forgets to proffer in moral form and which the wife consumes in physical form).

Everywhere they can, women seek gratification, looking after, reassurance. They will turn to an 'other' – a woman – to ask for a recipe, an address, the name of a remedy, anything; and they are accepted and understood. Recently this has assumed proportions that are alarming to men, who cannot understand how homosexuality could take the place of heterosexuality, and all on account of some stuff about feeling, some need for regression which seems to baffle them. Women are indeed turning to other women to be loved un-conditionally; without slavery, and with the right to regress.

If only men could view female demand differently; if only they could see that the need to be little is not exclusive to men or women, but represents those little recreations both need in order to fulfil adult roles the rest of the time. Regressing, going back in time, is the touchstone of our psychic lives, just as sleep is the return to begin-nings that is indispensable at the physical level. Why should women have to do without the means of living a healthy psychic life? Why should their only right to regress be indirect?

A woman goes to the hairdresser's: is it to satisfy her husband's wish for her to be beautiful, or her own wish to be petted and patted and fussed over, and not have anything else to think about for a couple of hours (always this strange flirting between her own desire and that of the other; always the duplicity of the woman, caught between what she is and what she is told to be)? You've met them too, just as I have, those women whose visit to the hairdresser's has transformed them for a few hours. There they felt that they were having a treat, or that they were treating themselves. Who will ever know? Who has been telling lies in all this? The women? The hair-dresser? The husband?

Read Gabrielle Rolin's *Chères menteuses* ('*dear liars*')[1] and you will find out all there is to know about the perpetual, inevitable lying that women do. But men don't want to know about or understand our lying; they want to pretend it has nothing to do with them. Above all they are anxious not to have feminine existence interfere with them in any way, while women see their world turned upside down and inside out by male existence.

And in fact, don't all divorces these days arise from a double life? Men have been unwilling to see women's need to regress; women have pretended to go along with that. But then suddenly women realize that they stand to gain nothing from these big, self-centred, demanding babies, and decide to leave (divorce at present is more often asked for by women than by men). The couple splits up over the matter of a regression shared out unequally between the partners; with his regression taking up the whole house, while hers amounts to no more than a few moments on the pillow (hence the disproportionate importance of the pillow, which the man with his usual fear of intimacy and words, can only partly recognize and accept). Women divorce more often than men, but most of the time it is because men have failed to ensure that the women have even one place where they can regress; or to realize that solitude inside marriage is no different from solitude outside it.

Are there still going to be women who accept that marriage should allow regression and sublimation to only one partner? Are they not proving that they prefer a life without any contract, since the contract always works against the freedom of the same partner?

12

The family: a modern theatre for an ancient play

We don't need mother and father any more. We only need mothering and fathering.
David Cooper, *The Death of the Family* (London, 1972), 29

Act 1: The absent father

Patriarchal society, Oedipal structure, nuclear family: this is the ground of the analyst's intervention. It is a ground where the analyst must face the question of the social dimension of the Oedipus complex, and of society as agent of neurosis.

With society evolving and yet not changing radically, there is a shift in prohibitions, and in symptoms as well. The days of hysterical acting-out are gone; what we have now is discreet psychosomatic conversion. With homosexuality already admitted as a possible form of sexuality, we are now witnessing the appearance of bisexuality. All of which means that the field of psychoanalysis is constantly shifting, but also that the unconscious is still one jump ahead of that special kind of investigator we call a psychoanalyst.

It is for example noteworthy that, with the shrinking of the family unit, the sharing out of roles between men and women has become more and more clearly defined; Oedipal issues have become more and more bound up with the mother; and the front page of newspapers has been taken over by sex and violence. If the ancient myth has the ill-fated hero go through the killing of his father and the illicit sexual relation with his mother, does the new, more intimate version of the family drama bring any refinement of that myth? Is there any relationship between the smaller, more close-knit family and the violence of feeling that arises when only father and mother are there to take the leading roles?

The more I read the papers, the more I experience family life, the more I listen to my patients, the more I find myself wondering whether my work might not be connected less with sick individuals than with a sick society. For the personal history of these patients is never more than a reflection of what they present in and through their symptoms; and their symptoms always follow on from the fact that they find it impossible to resolve a drama written for three actors but more often performed by two, with the father usually not on stage.

The image that the family has in the larger residential units is that of a minute cell in a giant social organism. The more the residential structure comes to matter, the more the family is confined within a few square yards. Within each of these tiny family worlds, one person reigns supreme: the mother. Every child's universe stretches only as far as its mother and its siblings, because, in the early days at least, it's the mother who usually takes on the baby-minding more or less permanently.

Since society provides no extra-family resources for children outside school hours (too few crèches or baby-minding services, virtually no premises for adolescents), one member of the couple has to be recognized as responsible for the child. As a matter of course it will be the mother, who, since she is on a lower salary scale than her husband, will feel no hesitation about coming forward as the one to give up working.

So it comes about that the child will spend most of its time alone with its mother, since the father is mostly away at work – 'gone car', as the child so rightly says. In this new consumer society, the missing figure is the father. What a strange society it is which, using the excuse that it is raising the level of material comfort via the father's salary, steps up psychic disturbance by way of an exclusively feminine upbringing and education. Not only do we have the absent father; we also have the permanently present mother.

There was a time when, if there was something that couldn't be said within the immediate family, it would be said somewhere else – to an uncle, a cousin, a neighbour. In the huge, extended society of those days, there was always someone in the 'family' one could fall back on. Nowadays, in this compartmentalized world of ours, the family, now reduced to its most basic form, is the only place where any talking can be done. Hence the increasing tension between parents and children. Too much is demanded of this mother, who, as a result, makes too many demands on her child. The whole thing is distressing precisely because it is unavoidable.

Since Oedipal feelings (running between the child and the parent of the opposite sex) cannot be given expression in so small a theatre, they will be acted out all the more violently in the future couple, in anything to do with love. The contraction of the family unit brings about a dramatizing of the affective conflicts normal in childhood. Love has been given undue importance, for the evidence is clear: it cannot mitigate what went wrong in infancy. And so we go in for divorce, because compromise seems impossible to this new generation, so fiercely single-minded, so violent.

Child-rearing looms large in the life of a woman. Feeling that she bears the entire responsibility for the child, she is ready to sacrifice everything for it – even if that means turning aggressive towards the child later on.

The Oedipus complex looks very different now that it is lived out in a sealed-off space, with mother and child forever face to face as the only actors in the drama. Inseparable, bound in alienation to each other. Think of how often we hear women saying of their child: 'He went and had measles on me' (did he fall ill to spite you?), or 'She came back to me with one out of ten for arithmetic' (does she go to school for her benefit or yours?).

Is there any limit to what the child can do 'to her'? It's quite simple: what this child has done is to be there all the time, so that there's no way of getting a single minute without it, so that the child is virtually riveted to the mother, so that it's all just too much for all concerned: for the mother, who becomes aggressive towards her beloved child; for the child, who has no freedom, since everything it does, it does 'to her'.

If there could be a different upbringing for children, where part of the responsibility was borne by outside agencies, mother and child would recover a degree of freedom: for a few hours at a time it would be possible for them to act in line with their own nature, not by reaction to the desire of the other.

What, in your view, is the commonest origin of those unhappy writing difficulties which are so often behind visits to the therapist? For children it is the impossibility of building up an 'I' independent of the 'she' of the mother, actually present within the child who is apparently in the classroom on its own. This child is never on its own: it is always connected to the mother, which leads to confusion both as to gender (masculine and feminine are inextricably intertwined), and as to number (how can it tell one from more-than-one when life with mother has always involved two people?). The child has no grasp of singular and plural. And yet there are people who are surprised, amazed even, at this lack of logic, which is entirely logical as far as the child is concerned. What the child knows is not 'one' but 'two', child and mother. That's how it's been since birth; why should things suddenly be different at school? (Do I need to say at this point that it is more often boys who come to see us with educational problems – no doubt because, living as they do close up to a mother-figure of the opposite sex, the whole question of genders gets mixed up in their head?)

And are we women analysts to spend our time repairing the damage caused by this minimal family unit, this upbringing left entirely in the hands of women, and not say anything about the social dimension? Are we to find ways of instilling or removing guilt (depending on what kind of analysts we are) in or from those mothers whose only experience is the infernal circle of masochism–devotion–aggressiveness, to which the child replies with refusal–aggressiveness–guilt?

Perhaps we are supposed not to notice that, for some time now, these mothers have been consulting us on their own, imagining themselves to be entirely responsible for the present situation, since they and they alone have shouldered the burden of the child. Surely we must rather tell them right away, as a first step, that bringing up a child is too heavy, too difficult a burden to be borne by one woman on her own, and that if the father is yet again not there in the consulting room, that doesn't mean that he's not implicated in the child's history that is being told there.

Ah, but there's a 'but': the man believes that fathering is a once-for-all business, and that he has been let off. His idea was that mothering would be enough now – and in any case, how could he find the time or the energy to do any other kind of fathering, when he's always so tired from his work outside? 'Oh, if I had to rely on *him* . . .', the women say triumphantly (the triumph is short lived, and dear bought), happy to see him kept out of a role where at last they can be better than the man. We have to consider the possibility that the child is a bastion for the woman in this unending sex war.

It does often look as if the fierce determination with which the woman lays claim to the child is only matched by that with which the man refuses to take it on.

But a new kind of woman has been appearing over the past few years: one who wants to live *with* her child, not *through* it. This new woman wants to go on being socially active even while she has young children. What she needs is to find structures or organizations which can take charge of the child beyond the end of school-time. A woman like this thinks of motherhood as one function among others, not as an end in itself. And in that case the child need not take the woman any further out of her way than it will take the man out of his. For, unless you're careful, motherhood, which should be no more than a stage on the woman's way, turns into a terminus.

When I, as a wife, a mother, a psychoanalyst question myself about the difficulties encountered in the course of my life, I find that they are all located in or round the mother; in or round that part of psychoanalytic theory that bears on women and the structure of their unconscious. For the business of motherhood is unbearable, buttressed as it is by a theory that is indefensible, in which Freud decides that I as a woman shall want a child as replacement for the penis that I never had. Well, I'm sorry, but this child has never blocked off from me the fact that I have to turn to the other sex to get back to wholeness. I note that men are in exactly the same situation, but that Freud didn't draw the same conclusions in their case – otherwise the child might have been held to be a replacement for what they lacked in the way of breasts and womb. The child could have represented for the couple the universal 'object' – which would put the child itself in a very different position, totally unrelated to the classic family pattern upheld by Freud, in which the child belongs to the mother.

In fact, like all of you, men and women alike, I wanted this child as the very image of man and woman together; as the outward and visible sign of the convergence of two different worlds. The desire for a child belongs to the world of reconciliation of the sexes, of bisexuality, but once born, the child is caught up in the sex war as a result of the fact that its upbringing is the business of one sex only. This child, symbol of the two-in-one, continuing embodiment of the union achieved momentarily in coitus, is, by reason of its prenatal sojourn inside a female body, annexed to the body of a particular woman. One might have imagined that this shared existence would be over after a few months, but, thanks to society, it will last a great deal longer than that! The cutting of the umbilical cord in no way breaks up the unity of mother and child, since society has planned it that way, and will do everything to keep it that way.

Between conception and birth, the desire for a child undergoes changes, in both men and women. By way of their pregnancy, the women seem to be moving towards the 'all', whereas the men feel left out of the project which they had conceived. When the birth takes place, men don't have the nerve to reclaim what is theirs, and women do nothing which might help them along. They will keep the child to themselves. Since men have to go without physical connectedness to the child during pregnancy, they won't go back to it after the birth. For the father, the child is part of the history of his line, his succession. But as for the history of the child's body, no, he'll have nothing to do with it: that history will unfold with the mother only.

The splitting in two of the child's world happens in the cradle, and it is there that the establishing of sexual identity begins to have overtones of sexism. For the child is working at establishing itself in a world where everything to do with body and feeling is linked to the mother, while anything like intellectual longings or the carrying on of the family line – and therefore of social position – is thought of as masculine. Right from the start, sexual difference affects not only the genital organs, as Freud pointed out, but everything. We are all of us creatures who take up sexual identity very early: this is the awkwardness that gets into the early life of the individual, preparing each and every one of us for what will become the sex war.

This child of mine that had been wanted by both of us – what a burden he was as soon as he'd emerged from his dwelling inside me! In there he was no trouble at all. He let me live my life, he went everywhere with me. But, as soon as he was born, he started to cling to me: I was all he had, his one recourse, his one and only mother. What a yawning gap there was between the dream of something achieved by both of us, my husband and myself, and the enormous burden which, all of a sudden, fell to me and me only!

Only then did I realize that society was not planned for us, that is, the child and me. Only for my husband. Is this some all-male society which I happened to blunder into, as the result of some oversight or omission? Is this not all part of what I hear even now from men – or psychoanalysts: 'Penisless' woman, make the most of your phallic child, and think of it as the 'object' that you lack. That's your only chance, your only achievement, the only position you'll be helped to take up, for everything else belongs to men.

If I take a look at my life as a woman, I notice that the fact that I had a recognized job gave me no right to any help from society in the upbringing of my children. On the contrary: no effort was spared to impress on me that the care of the child came first. Welfare benefits were paid for out of the husband's salary as sole earner, and at a rate that took no account of the family's standard of living. As for my work, well, that was merely optional (there could be no financial assistance for having the child looked after, unless my living standard was abnormally low). These few indications tell the tale: the rearing of children, at home, by the mother is first and foremost a choice made by governments. It is not enough to say that mothers have the possibility of stopping work. For the most part, they have no possibility of doing anything else.

Ever since we were tiny, society has been casting us by sex in roles that leave no room for initiative or manoeuvre – so much so that we sometimes have difficulty in getting a clear sense of our own desire. It is unthinkable for a woman not to fuss over babies; it is laughable if a man dares to enjoy fussing over them.

Since it had all been more or less set up from outside, I had to do my bit of fussing and cuddling, and, since I also wanted to go on working, I came up against the awful dilemma that faces so many women. No-one would stand in for me when I couldn't be there; there were no arrangements outside the family to have the baby minded until I had finished work. There can't be anyone left who is unaware that crèches and baby-minding services are, in the light of current needs, practically non-existent. I lived in a town with a population of 140,000. In it there was a grand total of two crèches and one short-term baby-minding service. Nothing for it, then, but the fall-back solutions, the more or less ingenious arrangements with the grandmother or the woman next door, and so on. Nothing for it but to feel, by mid-afternoon each day, the awful anxiety of knowing that the little darlings had left a totally organized world for a totally unorganized one. Four o'clock: a bad moment for most women, with another hour of work still to go, an hour which they must also live through as anxious mothers. 'Maybe it won't all work out right today. Oh, don't let anything awful have happened. Please let life and health just go on ticking over as smoothly and as regularly as the hands on the clock!' – these are the sorts of thoughts women start having after four o'clock. But what kind of government is it that won't face the fact that, among women employees, efficiency and productivity fall as maternal guilt and anxiety rise?

I have waited and waited, but to no avail (it used to be men ministers, then it was women ministers); without ever hearing any mention of this serious problem of child-minding and maternal anxiety. Perhaps we ought to have psychoanalysts in the ministries of Health and Education? For now that women have made up their minds that their child is no longer going to be an obstacle in their path, they are having to go in for ever more elaborate contortions to cover the ground between office and cradle.

Nothing has been done to make it possible to go in for reproduction and at the same time carry on working. No wonder the enthusiasts for a high birth-rate policy feel put out! As long as society doesn't step in to help the two parents by accepting part of the responsibility for minding the young child, there will go on being fewer children.

Tying the mother to her child by means of a salary (the solution usually adopted by the pro-family lobby) is no way to solve the problem of the woman enslaved by her child. The way to give her back the sense that procreation goes with joy, not sorrow, is to relieve her of the burden of sole charge. Yes, the family is shrinking, and it will go on shrinking if the people at the top in this society of ours don't make every effort to ensure that motherhood is not seen any longer as an end in itself, but as one function among others; one that doesn't block off all others, one that has no more disruptive an effect on the woman's road than fatherhood has on the man's.

It is within maternity, not sexuality, that the main inequity between the sexes lies. Man, excluded from pregnancy, has decided to take revenge for this intense and unshareable female involvement by keeping away from the child, not just for nine months, but for nine years and more. For years and years, then, the woman must carry on her own the fruit of the desire of both partners.

Man passes through fatherhood; woman gets stuck in motherhood. She is locked away, socially, in what was, once upon a time, her own desire; while the man escapes scot-free. Motherhood thus becomes a social choice, which results in the disappearance of the woman and the birth of the mother along with the child. Is it surprising that, faced with a choice of this sort, there are women who give up along the way? Is it surprising that, caught between the deep, instinctive desire of two people to have a child and the birth that she must go through alone, a woman may set up the guillotine of abortion between the dream and the reality?

'The desire for a child' and 'motherhood' are two such different entities that, if both men and women fall to dreaming over the former, the woman, faced with the latter, very often wakes up alone, needing to take decisions that are a scandal to the man, who is still dreaming. Dreaming of the child which he hasn't the power to keep, since he didn't have the courage to take responsibility for it.

It is staggering to see how persistent men are in wanting to keep alive children which they will never have to look after (I have in mind here what amounts to the general opposition of French doctors to abortion!).

Act 2: The mother's sacrifice

Maternity, in itself a change of physiological state, becomes a change of social status as well. Wherever there is maternity, there comes an inescapable choice: either of giving up the status of woman and taking on that of mother – which may well produce an impression of immediate contentment, to be followed, a few years later on, by a great many disappointments, when the woman wants to go back to living a normal life; or else of keeping her status as woman and being a mother as well. This produces an immediate impression of stress and strain, often accompanied by guilt, but keeps a place in society for the woman, who will not feel useless when her children move on.

By coming into the world at all, the child affects the internal balance of his mother so much that the consequences are bound to be felt on both sides of the relationship. The mother's love will often be ambivalent, the child's love often tinged with anxiety, and guilt, even opposition to this aggressiveness in the mother.

Possibility A. If the woman has chosen to stay at home with her child, because this solution in her view is more to her advantage financially and psychologically, the child becomes actively involved in the libidinal economy of the mother. The child will be the living proof of her success, there in person to indicate that she really is a good mother. The child here is 'that-which-is-paid-to-the-mother' – her salary. There is nothing a child in that position can do or want that will not be for or against her. The child feels itself to be carrying on its shoulders an existence which is not its own. And that is sometimes a burden so heavy that quite a few of the ones I see would prefer to go back to where they came from.

The mothers who say 'You're killing me' or 'You'll be the death of me' reveal by these words that their very existence is now linked with and dependent on the child. And which of us, whether child or adult, would want to carry within us the success or failure of someone else?

When the sacrosanct Mother's Day comes round, what we see, don't we, is a reference to the scale of the maternal sacrifices, and the need for reparative gestures towards these women who have done so much for their children. Mothers must indeed feel they are exploited, devalued, debased, when we find them so ready to accept a big build-up on that one day! If these mothers who stay at home with their child get such intense pleasure from doing so, what need is there to thank them? The only people who are granted rehabilitation are those who have suffered injury or damage. It is no accident that this revaluation has gone to mothers first!

I myself wanted children for pleasure. I would hate them to have to thank me for the joy I feel, the joy we have found in making them and watching them grow! Should I not be the one to do the thanking, or to apologize to them for having entered their names in the book of life without consulting them, all because I didn't want my life to come to a dead end one day?

Possibility B. Suppose, however, that the woman has decided to carry on down her own road and keep her place in society, in the conviction that motherhood is not the whole of her destiny. She will very soon learn that there has been no material provision for her child. Nor will it be long before she is plunged into anxiety and guilt. At the child's first illness, the mother's life is transformed into a hell of worry. The biggest criticism of working women is that absenteeism is rife, in the form of sick leave, which invariably masks the illness of another person: the child.

These women describe themselves as computers forever on-line. And indeed several unrelated programmes are running in their heads at any one time. Two lives, two faces, two smiles, two anxieties – everything gets doubled in the life of any woman who works and has a child. How enviable the man's life-style then seems: only one programme in his head at any one time, only one salary, paid exclusively into his hand or into his bank – how simple it all seems!

Women swing about between one status and the other. Most have tried out both at one time or another. But there's always something that goes wrong with the system, and that something is always the mother's taking on the care of the child on her own, with every intention of going on with it. So deep and so early is her conditioning to this that she believes that that's the way her own worth is established. Not for a moment does it occur to her to share with the man the one role he has handed over to her entirely. And the man, delighted at finding such a reliable baby-sitter for his child – why would he want to go persuading her into a different job-distribution? Thus it comes about, that when the woman has a job, she still, unlike the man, keeps her family role as the one who looks after the child.

As long as women haven't got beyond feeling personally guilty, as long as they go on putting more value on other people than on themselves, men, who are not fools, will go on making the most of this appalling weakness. They will be careful, of course, to trick it out with the grandest of names: maternal devotion, feminine instinct, visceral bondedness. Behind all these grand words there is always some kind of rehabilitation going on. Women are being given back all the freedom they've lost – but only in the form of praise-earning maternity. The fact that the mother's freedom has become the other's freedom will be called 'devotion'.

All this devotion, renunciation, abdication: somehow or other the child is going to have to pay for them. It is such a heavy burden, being the child of this woman who needs above all justification and gratification! When the sacrifice of the one has been duly recorded in the heart of the other, does it not create between them a sort of unpardonable debt between generations? When a woman exerts domination over creatures who are young and unable to defend themselves, is she not likely to find herself later on faced with resentment from children and adults of both sexes? As we have seen, the man will get his revenge by pushing her out of all his territories, while the daughter's immutable view of her is of a rival. These are paltry thanks, are they not, for someone who has 'done so much' for her child. Motherhood, it must be clear, is a snare which brings women, in exchange for a few years of joy mixed with pain, a lifetime of love mixed with hate from those we live with.

I cannot fail to notice that every neurosis rests in the first instance on the relation with the mother, perceived as taking up the whole front of the stage, for child and adult alike. For me as a woman, that is a destiny (if we could only be sure it really was one) which is heavy to bear. Women ought to be the first to get away from the burning heat, the riskiness of being stage front. Is it not alarming to find out that, as long as women bring up children on their own, whatever sort of life they actually work out with their children, they will be held responsible for everything that happens to those children?

It is surely dreadful to have to pay so dear and for so long for the joy that we made a point of keeping to ourselves. The Oedipal sequence as it unfolds in present-day society makes woman into the only target for the ancient resentment experienced towards the mother. If we want to do anything about the come-uppance regularly inflicted on women in social terms, must we not first of all prevent infantile resentment from being directed exclusively at them within the family?

This place that the mother has, which we are told is so enviable, is surely rather more like a minefield. And then this no man's land that lies between us and the infant at birth: we might be well advised to cross it together, man and woman, each leaving behind a mark different from the other.

Let the feminine world stop being the only reference-point by which the child of either sex finds its bearings; let the man take a part in the psychic formation of his child, as he did in its conception. Then his son may experience similarity right from the start, instead of having to cling desperately to a dissimilarity with the woman which will damage his relationship with her as an adult. Then his daughter may, from the outset, be able to see herself in a mirror held by the opposite sex, which reveals her body as desirable, and not need any longer to keep scanning her image in the eyes of the man who is to come – and who seems unable to appease his partner's anxiety. The mother seen as bringing castration by her presence, the father described as bringing salvation by his absence: these are dire images for both members of the couple, and it is not easy to get away from them.

All in all, the attempt to lock up the woman has had the effect of locking everybody up: the whole family bears the mark of her sacrifice. Has there been any serious appreciation of the influence of this woman, pronounced 'feminine' and 'gentle' on the basis of total ignorance about what she is actually like? It is becoming clearer that in reality she is neither of these things. How could she be 'feminine' and 'gentle', this woman who has been locked away, walled up within her femaleness from the very start of her existence? How could a prisoner (who has done nothing other than be born with a woman's sex) be gentle and happy at seeing the fate that was in store for her?

How can I myself, so familiar with individual neurosis, remain indifferent in face of the same neurosis lived out collectively? How can I not say that the main outcomes of the contemporary family are misogyny in men, and guilt in women? These are to be found even in the most trivial of newspaper articles, the least significant of parliamentary bills on family matters.

Act 3: Socio-political speech (in place of the chorus of classical antiquity)

The man issues the law which will lock the woman away, and the woman agrees to everything that suits the man, so concerned is she with not upsetting him, so accustomed has she been since infancy to fitting in with whatever image she is presented with, whatever role she is expected to take on.

What do we see in social terms if not that, whatever the political set-up, the woman's future is always made contingent on the child's? And if and when there are difficulties over the child, she will be immediately chained down. Let's say there aren't enough crèches and child-minding services. Fine, we'll arrange for the woman a period of maternity leave long enough to cover up the shortages in collective provision. We might even propose a salary, to be paid to the mother with three or more children (the solution considered by Michel Debré[1] as encouraging a higher birth-rate). At one stroke this would on the one hand obviate the necessity to provide public facilities for children, and, on the other, save the State from having to pay high salaries to child specialists. At an infinitely lower price, the mother would take on the whole rearing and early education of her own child – and there would be no danger of any strikes here, since employer and employee are in the same family.

Because it happens that our own dear leader, President Valéry Giscard d'Estaing, has a markedly Oedipal disposition, and we are now entitled to two years of maternity leave – to make sure that we get really involved in our child's Oedipal feelings, and for that reason, keep out of the social field. The President is no psychoanalyst: he has no notion of how phallocrats are made or women-as-objects born. His conscience is innocently untroubled by the fact that, even though he takes a public stance on the importance of involving women in politics, he too has found a way of keeping them off stage for a few years longer. The man can go in for trade union activities; 'she' will do the baby-sitting. There's no way round this: as long as we haven't disentangled the destiny of the child from that of the mother by providing outside help, women will be unable to break through to any masculine concerns and responsibilities. The world will go on being idiotically cut in two, society will go on being profoundly sexist, and destiny will go on being attributed to cradle-experience.

It looks as if men, on the right or on the left, have only one idea: to trick and imprison women, whether by way of appeals to duty or by money. They want to buy women's devotion, pay them for the love they lavish on their child. But do love and devotion have to go hand in hand? Is it not possible to love without going in for outsize, total self-sacrifice, as women do?

Politicians are not the only men to be victims of their Oedipal constitution. There are also all the male child specialists, experts on the birth-rate, scientific historians, editors of the major women's magazines (almost always men) who have a hand in the dissemination of sociological research. All of them are following the intricate steps in the long dance of the phallocrats who have been brought up by a woman, and before they've drawn breath, they're asking to have things go on in the same way for the next generation.

Let us look at the demands put forward by Mr P. Chaunu, a professor of modern history, in an article published in *Marie-France* in January 1978, under the heading: 'Are there too many of us or too few?' He first shows concern at the fall in the birth-rate, and asks society as a whole to make a general effort. But just watch how, very soon, very neatly, this general effort gets loaded on to women in the first instance. His idea, which is not new, is for the woman to bring up her child on her own from birth to age 3 or 5. Calling her by some grand name like 'private tutor' will make little difference to the mother's situation, or her enslavement; but this time the proposal is more insidiously dangerous, and may well lure a number of women into the trap laid by men.

Mr Chaunu calls insistently for a 'maternal' salary (why maternal? Has the father got something terrible wrong with him that keeps him out of this function?) for three years or five years for all women, who could then choose to become children's nurse and nursery-school teacher to their own children. ('Choose'? Are you sure that, in a social system where some couples have barely £250 a month to live on, any extra money wouldn't be seen as an 'obligation'? Have we laboured long and hard to get clear of the child-as-accident, all in order to bring in now the child-as-source-of-gain? Are women never to feel free in their desire for motherhood?) Only this financial provision can offer a basis for genuine equality between the sexes. (No, Mr Chaunu. Since the plan is to offer this salary to the woman only, I fail to see how it restores the equality of the sexes; on the contrary. What I can see is how it 'disequals' them in face of the child. And if women's maternal function is equal to men's, why do men seem in no hurry to take it on?)

Furthermore: pension rights for mothers of three or more children, the only way to fight against the injustice of a society where everybody benefits from provision of this kind except mothers – those who have borne in their hearts and in their flesh the generation that will pay for these pensions.

Our relation to our mother is weighed down already by many things: do you want to turn it into a hell on earth, by adding the 'good repayments' now required of adults to the good behaviour that used to be required of children? Is it your wish that this earliest of all relations should amount to no more than debts, duties, and obligations? Why mix up a mother's love with the work a child makes? Any child who is not a stranger to its mother belongs to the world of love, not the world of salaries. Whereas the child who is a stranger to its teacher moves out of the area of desire into that of education. Teachers have always been paid, as far as I know, but I very much hope that parents will never be. That would be the start of something I don't dare put a name to, and it would be the end of love. Having a child is a present which parents give each other, and it is beyond price because it is unique. Does this present seem so poisoned that neither men nor women could want it without prompting?

What nobody wants is total charge of this child. What everyone wants is the love of this child. So it is plain that the charge must be divided up differently, by opening short-term baby-minding services, by paying crèche supervisors and nursery-school teachers who can look after the child. By introducing greater flexibility into holiday dates, so that parents can take over from each other. If once there is a move to offer payment for a function as instinctive as having a child, it's hard to see what parts of human life would not be subject to payment.

There are so many pleasures that cannot be obtained without some effort beforehand. The child is, in the first instance, the parents' pleasure, and there can be no question of parents ever having children because it's good for society; only because it's good for them.

If the charge of the child does harm, in particular to the mother, then that is what we must work at if we are to affect the birth-rate. The child must not be a cage – even a gilded one – for the mother.

Fortunately, not everybody has the same outlook as Mr Chaunu: buying citizens by paying parents seems not to be quite so obvious a solution as that gentleman would have us believe. In the same magazine, another researcher, Mr Leridon takes up his pen (and here I have to give credit to *Marie-France*) to say:

> Since no. 3 is unwanted, all is surely not well with no. 2. The first step should be to analyse these difficulties. Once the explanation of a problem has been found, experience shows that the problem ceases to exist.

But I don't believe that the problem of the falling birth-rate will simply cease to exist, for there is obviously widespread reluctance to trace the question back to causes. There is a clear wish to leave the child in the hands of the mother. The real problem is that this child bars the mother's way, forcing her to give up her own development in favour of someone else's. It is this which some women are now starting to reckon the cost of, just as they are starting to understand that, if they have in the past gone along with this system, it is on account of their guilt-feelings, which make them believe in the value of the other more than in their own.

By accepting the role of mother devoted to her children, the woman is still secretly hoping to get back to the norm, to be a real woman (as we know, that has been her main objective since her earliest days), recognized as 'satisfactory' in the eyes of other people. Within motherhood, women are still, as ever, in pursuit of their image. But is this the only favourable image of themselves that they can aspire to having? In a patriarchal society, the man sets the woman up in the home with the children, so that he may hold sway everywhere else. Must women take as their true vocation what is merely the man's wish?

Anyhow, Mr Leridon raises the problem, and a few lines later on he writes: 'To live in any other way would involve giving everyone his or her chance.' I am supposing that motherhood is not, for the woman, the only chance. She should be free to choose another chance if she so desires, but obviously that would entail that the child would be taken on either by the partner or by agencies outside the family. Giving the child its chance doesn't necessarily mean forcing it to live through the one-to-one with its mother; we have seen how much it can suffer at her hands.

But, as Mr Leridon again admits: 'In general, we have to recognize that our society is totally unfit for children, and takes no account of their specific needs.' It is indeed true that society is more interested in money, that is, in material comforts, than in the psychic health of individuals. True also that no-one knows exactly how to deal with the specific needs of children. Should they be brought up separately, or collectively? Should they be fondled and handled by men? or by women? In a relation to their mother that is exclusive? or partial? There are still no answers other than the good old Church-and-State one: women and children at home.

Sure enough, a woman analyst can't even have a quiet read of a woman's magazine without coming across the seeds of the Oedipal dead-ends which form the locus of her professional intervention. But then, to open one of these magazines is to come up straightaway against the two stereotypes that have been the undoing of women. There is the woman-as-object, who must be attractive to men (by way of fashion); and there is the woman whose object is her child (sociological articles presenting the child as the woman's responsibility).

It is surely the analyst's duty to say that the mother image in analysis is usually as overdeveloped as the part she played in the subject's real life. And to include the reminder that this individual whom we believe we can help comes from a society about which we as analysts say little or nothing.

The Oedipal poison has spilled over everything, and unbeknown to us, Oedipal thinking is so deeply embedded in us that we no longer notice its effects. The 'Oedipalizing' of society is widespread. Are we not forced to say that that process follows from the law of the father and the upbringing given by the mother? That this feminine upbringing gives rise, in her sons, to an anti-feminine law which is necessarily cruel to women? And therefore that every patriarchal society of itself secretes the anti-feminine ferment?

It can hardly be questioned that, for men, the main goal is preventing women from existing as equals or superiors. If feminists today are fighting, it is to recover the right to an existence, but, I repeat, they are in my view focusing their attack on the surface layer of sexism, its secondary effects, whereas the sexist phenomenon has been rooted in men's hearts since earliest infancy. That is where it can be spotted – and where something can be done about it. Only by retreating from the nursery, and letting men in, will women have any chance of seeing a let-up in the sex war.

And there you have my answer to the question I asked at the outset: how far can a woman analyst be a feminist? Certainly not all the way, to the place where women are fighting now, because the men whom they are talking to, the men they want to convince, have long since closed their ears to any words that might have come from women. A woman analyst may have dealings with feminism in so far as she finds it appropriate to give an account of a sexism which, directed against women, comes into being in the cradle, and has its roots deep in the unconscious.

Psychoanalysis will make its contribution to feminism via the extent to which it can make conscious and explicable a conflict between the sexes that has hitherto been unconscious and inexplicable. *Wo es war, soll Ich werden.* (That has been the aim of psychoanalysis ever since Freud.)

With family patterns as they are at the moment, the unconscious can only be structured by reference to the mother, the only person felt by the child to be doing the rearing. Later on, as a result, each person's conscious seeks to square its accounts with the woman, who is thus at the receiving end of the vengefulness of both sexes.

Here men and women must stop and see how much the privileges granted to mothers turn into evil spells which pursue women without respite all the rest of their lives. It is essential for women to realize that if they hold on to power over this infant, they will automatically be kept out of any other form of power.

The new women are those who no longer confuse motherhood with property, or role with vocation, and who intend to take an active part in production as well as reproduction, whereas, up till now, we had believed that we were only entitled to one or the other, according to sex.

Full existence for women depends on a prior desacralizing of the mother, whose long reign has given rise to misogyny in men and jealousy in women. It is possible for there to be another family, another upbringing and education, another way of dividing up social and parental tasks, such that children could meet, from the moment they appear in the world, a same-sex referent and a complement from the other sex. The one would offer a basis for identification, while the other would ensure access to the Oedipal stage and to identity. As long as the family remains the site of difference between man's role and woman's role, children will find in it the seeds of sexism.

Men and women must agree to take on role equality within sexual difference, so that the child may understand that differences of body do not entail differences of power, a concept basic to the current war between the sexes.

Beginnings . . .

Read Sophocles, read Freud, discover this astonishing truth: no-one can escape the Oracle, no-one can escape desire.

Today's women, in spite of all they've read (and in particular the text they're reading now), will be unable to turn their backs on their own desire for the 'other' sex, any more than Jocasta, in spite of warnings, could avoid marrying her own son.

Up till now it has always been the man who tries to run away. Like Laius on his chariot, he tries to avoid desire and encounters death.

For ages it has been the man who leaves the home and the woman who stays there, shouldering all the burden the ancients knew, and in addition, guilt. But things can change; perhaps the 'other history' is about to start . . .

What will men do, if we too turn our backs on our desire – which is to conceive, to bear, to go on – if we decide to give up motherhood so as not to carry the weight of guilt?

If men refuse to take responsibility for the consequences of their wish for a child, why should we answer its inarticulate cries?

Laius, don't go, don't leave me alone, with just 'him' facing 'her', or else all he'll dream about will be marrying me and then killing me – you know he will . . . 'She' won't stop calling for you, searching for you, to pin you down, to keep you . . . Come, Laius, this is the start of another time; that elsewhere where the other will no longer be condemned to death[1] is already here with us, and it is you and I who are writing it.

Notes

Voices off

1 In a number of instances, Christiane Olivier has given no indications of source. Where she is quoting from a recognizable work, the reference is easily supplied. Where, as in this instance, she is quoting from a less identifiable source (presumably one of Freud's countless letters), it has not always been possible to locate the quotation. It should be said – the book itself will make this abundantly clear – that Mme Olivier sees pedantry as a characteristically male trap. She does, however, give some references, and since in any case translation brings a new situation, I have decided to give references where possible; in detail for texts published in English or already translated, less precisely for texts not already translated (translator's note).

2 François Roustang, *Dire Mastery* (*Un Destin si funeste*), trans. Ned Lukacher (Baltimore, 1982), 70.

3 Robert Stoller in *Nouvelle revue de psychanalyse* (Paris, 1973), no. 7. (Here and subsequently, translations not otherwise attributed are my own.)

4 Luce Irigaray, *This Sex Which is Not One* (*Ce Sexe qui n'en est pas un*), trans. Catherine Porter and Carolyn Burke (New York, 1985), 86.

5 Robert Pujol, 'La mère au féminin', in *Nouvelle revue de psychanalyse* (Paris, 1977), no. 16.

6 Hélène Cixous, *The Newly Born Woman* (*La Jeune née*), trans. Betsy Wing (Manchester, 1986), 68.

7 Pujol, *op. cit.*

8 Cixous, *op. cit.*, 67.

9 Jacques Lacan, quoted in Juliet Mitchell and Jacqueline Rose, *Feminine Sexuality* (London, 1982), 144. The extracts from Lacan are translated by Jacqueline Rose.

10 Cixous, *op. cit.*, 67.

11 Jacques Lacan in Mitchell and Rose: *op. cit.*, 145.

12 Cixous, *op. cit.*, 68.

13 Irigaray, *op. cit.*, 212.

14 Anaïs Nin: see note 1. This passage would seem to be taken from her *Journals*, but does not correspond exactly to anything in any of them.
15 Cixous, *op. cit.*, 97.

1 The conspiracy of silence

1 Sophocles, *Oedipus the King* in David Grene and Richmond Lattimore (eds), *The Complete Greek Tragedies* (3 vols, Chicago, 1959), II, 57.
2 Luce Irigaray, *Speculum of the Other Woman* (*Speculum, de l'autre femme*), trans. Gillian C. Gill (New York, 1985), 55.
3 Germaine Greer, *The Female Eunuch* (London, 1970), 55.
4 Unless otherwise indicated, all quotations from or details of Freud's work are taken from *The Standard Edition of the Complete Psychological Works of Sigmund Freud*, under the general editorship of James Strachey (24 vols, London, 1953–74), henceforward referred to as *S.E.* The studies alluded to here are: 'Analysis of a phobia in a five-year-old boy' (*S.E.* X, 5–119); 'Leonardo da Vinci and a memory of his childhood' (*S.E.* XI, 63–137); 'Psychoanalytic notes on an autobiographical account of a case of paranoia' (*S.E.* XII, 9–82); and *Moses and Monotheism* (*S.E.* XXIII, 3–127).
5 In *Letters of Sigmund Freud*, ed. Ernst L. Freud, trans. Tania and James Stern (London, 1961), 91.
6 Benoîte Groult, *Ainsi soit-elle* (Paris, 1977).
7 Freud, *S.E.* XX, 248.
8 Freud, *S.E.* XXI, 228.
9 Hélène Cixous, *The Newly Born Woman* (*La Jeune née*), trans. Betsy Wing (Manchester, 1986).

2 In the beginning was Freud

1 Sigmund Freud, *S.E.* VII, 195.
2 ibid.
3 ibid., 219.
4 ibid.
5 ibid., 195.
6 Freud, *S.E.* XIX, 252.
7 ibid., 253–4.
8 Luce Irigaray, *Speculum of the Other Woman* (*Speculum, de l'autre femme*), trans. Gillian C. Gill (New York, 1985).
9 ibid,. 51–2.
10 Annie Leclerc, *Parole de Femme* (Paris, 1975).
11 ibid.
12 ibid.
13 Freud, *S.E.* VII, 220–1.
14 Irigaray, *op. cit.*, 48.
15 Freud, *S.E.* VII, 221.

16 Irigaray, *op. cit.*, 71–2.
17 Jacques Lacan, in Juliet Mitchell and Jacqueline Rose, *Feminine Sexuality* (London, 1982), 146.
18 Lacan, in Mitchell and Rose, *op. cit.*, 145.
19 Freud, *S.E.* VII, 221.
20 Shere Hite, *The Hite Report* (New York, 1977).
21 Freud, *S.E.* XXII, 135.

3 Dark continent or blank page?

1 Sigmund Freud, *S.E.* XX, 212.
2 Jacques Lacan, in Juliet Mitchell and Jacqueline Rose, *Feminine Sexuality* (London, 1982), 144.
3 Freud, *S.E.* XXI, 226.
4 ibid., 228–9.
5 Sophocles: *Oedipus the King* in David Grene and Richmond Lattimore (eds), *The Complete Greek Tragedies* (3 vols, Chicago, 1959), II, 57.
6 Freud, *S.E.* XIX, 179.
7 Freud, *S.E.* XXI, 235.
8 ibid., 230.
9 Freud, *S.E.* XIX, 251.
10 Freud, *S.E.* XXI, 225.
11 Freud, *S.E.* XIX, 249.
12 Mustapha Safouan, *La Sexualité féminine dans la doctrine freudienne* (Paris, 1976).
13 Robert Pujol, 'La mère au feminin', in *Nouvelle revue de psychanalyse* (Paris, 1977).
14 ibid.
15 Lacan, in Mitchell and Rose, *op. cit.*, 144.
16 Pujol, *op. cit.*
17 Wladimir Granoff, *La Pensée et le féminin* (Paris, 1976).
18 Freud, *S.E.* XXI, 226–7.
19 See Voices off, note 1.
20 ibid.
22 Ruth Mack Brunswick, in Janine Chasseguet-Smirgel (ed.) *La Sexualité féminine* (Paris, 1976).
23 Freud, *S.E.* XXI, 226–7.
24 Janine Chasseguet-Smirgel in *Nouvelle revue de psychanalyse* (Paris, 1975), nos 1–2.
25 François Roustang, *Dire Mastery* (*Un Destin si funeste*), trans. Ned Lukacher (Baltimore, 1982).

4 Oedipal difference: where the trouble starts

1 Sigmund Freud, *S.E.* XXI, 226.
2 Freud, *S.E.* XX, 210.

3 ibid., 36.
4 ibid., 37.
5 Freud, *S.E.* XXI, 225.
6 ibid., 225.
7 Freud, *S.E.* XIX, 251.
8 Freud, *S.E.* XXI, 229.
9 Freud, *S.E.* XV, 207.
10 Freud, *S.E.* VII, 223.
11 Bella Grumberger, in Janine Chasseguet-Smirgel (ed.) *La Sexualité féminine* (Paris, 1976).
12 Elena Gianini Belotti, *Du Côté des petites filles* (Paris, 1976).

5 Anatomy or destiny?

1 Robert Stoller, in *Nouvelle revue de psychanalyse* (Paris, 1973), no. 7.
2 Elena Gianini Belotti, *Du Côté des petites filles* (Paris, 1976).
3 O. Brunet and I. Lézine, *Le Développement psychologique de la première enfance* (Paris, 1965).
4 Brunet and Lézine, *op. cit.*
5 ibid.
6 Gianini Belotti, *op. cit.*
7 Brunet and Lézine, *op. cit.*

6 A childhood memory

1 See Voices off, note 1. Madame de Ségur was the author of edifying works directed at children.

7 The featureless desert

1 On these customs see Margaret Mead, *From the South Seas* (New York, 1939).
2 See Annie Leclerc, *Parole de Femme* (Paris, 1975).

8 The spider's web

1 At the risk of seeming repetitious, I go on here to restate a number of points developed earlier. I do so, not from any want of confidence in the reader, but so that I can group these points together, in order to bring out more clearly the way in which male psychology is built up.

9 The impossible encounter

1 Paul Verlaine, 'Mon rêve familier', in *Oeuvres poétiques complètes*

(Paris, 1962). A plain prose rendering would give: 'I often have this strange, affecting dream of an unknown woman, who loves me and whom I love, and who each time is neither quite the same nor quite other.'

10 Words or war

1 On this see Marina Yaguello, *Les Mots et les femmes* (Paris, 1979).
2 On this see Alain Laurent, *Féminin masculin* (Paris, 1975): an amusing and shrewd presentation of male and female qualities and defects.
3 Hélène Cixous, *The Newly Born Woman* (*La Jeune née*), trans. Betsy Wing (Manchester, 1986).
4 Wladimir Granoff, *La Pensée et le féminin* (Paris, 1976).
5 Jacques Lacan, in Juliet Mitchell and Jacqueline Rose, *Feminine Sexuality* (London, 1982), 144.
6 The German word 'Neid' is used to indicate 'lack of', 'wish for'.
7 See Gabrielle Rolin, *Chères menteuses* ('dear liars'), (Paris, 1978).
8 Annie Leclerc, *Parole de femme* (Paris, 1975).
9 Henri de Montherlant, *La Reine morte* ('The dead queen'), in *Théâtre* (Paris, 1965).
10 On this see Luce Irigaray, *This Sex Which Is Not One* (*Ce Sexe qui n'en est pas un*), trans. Catherine Porter and Carolyn Burke (New York, 1985).
11 Montherlant, *op. cit.*
12 Sophocles, *Oedipus at Colonus*, in David Grene and Richmond Lattimore (eds), *The Complete Greek Tragedies* (3 vols, Chicago, 1959), II, 91.
13 See Voices off, note 1.
14 On this see Elena Gianini Belotti, *Du Côté des petites filles* (Paris, 1976).

11 Travelling light

1 Gabrielle Rolin, *Chères menteuses* ('dear liars'), (Paris, 1978).

12 The family: a modern theatre for an ancient play

1 Michel Debré was, at the time of publication of *Les Enfants de Jocaste*, a prominent political figure in France (former Prime Minister). He was a frequent commentator on social matters.

Beginnings . . .

1 Hélène Cixous, *The Newly Born Woman* (*La Jeune née*), trans. Betsy Wing (Manchester, 1986), 97.